GREAT PAINTINGS FROM THE PUSHKIN MUSEUM, MOSCOW

GREAT PAINTINGS

FROM THE

pushkin
museum

MOSCOW

TEXT BY K. M. MALITSKAYA, *Curator of Western European Art*

INTRODUCTION BY I. ANTONOVA, *Director*

HARRY N. ABRAMS, INC. *Publishers* NEW YORK

TRANSLATED BY NORBERT GUTERMAN

Library of Congress Catalog Card Number: 64–15232

All rights reserved. No part of the contents of this book may be reproduced without the permission of the publishers, Harry N. Abrams, Incorporated, New York.

Colorplates printed in Italy, text printed in Holland. Bound in West Germany

Reproduction rights reserved by A.D.A.G.P., Paris

TABLE OF CONTENTS

DUTCH SCHOOL

42. HENDRICK VAN AVERCAMP — *Skaters*
43. WILLEM CLAESZ. HEDA — *Still Life with Ham and Silver*
44. JAN VAN GOYEN — *The River Waal Near Niemegen*
45. SALOMON VAN RUYSDAEL — *Landscape with River*
46. PIETER CODDE — *The Concert*
47. ADRIAEN VAN OSTADE — *The Flute Player*
48. REMBRANDT VAN RIJN — *Ahasuerus, Haman, and Esther*
49. REMBRANDT VAN RIJN — *Portrait of Adriaen van Rijn, the Artist's Brother*
50. REMBRANDT VAN RIJN — *Portrait of an Old Woman*
51. EMANUEL DE WITTE — *Waterfront Market*
52. PIETER DE HOOCH — *Young Man Dressing*
53. JACOB VAN RUISDAEL — *View of the Village of Egmont*

ENGLISH SCHOOL

54. THOMAS LAWRENCE — *Portrait of Sally Siddons*
55. THOMAS LAWRENCE — *Portrait of Countess Vorontsova*
56. JOHN CONSTABLE — *View of Highgate*

FRENCH SCHOOL

57. NICOLAS POUSSIN — *Joshua's Victory Over the Amorites*
58. CLAUDE LORRAIN — *The Rape of Europa*
59. ANTOINE WATTEAU — *Satire on Physicians*
60. FRANÇOIS LEMOYNE — *The Rape of Europa*
61. FRANÇOIS BOUCHER — *Hercules and Omphale*
62. JEAN-BAPTISTE-SIMÉON CHARDIN — *The Attributes of the Arts*
63. JEAN-HONORÉ FRAGONARD — *Savoyard with Kerchief*
64. JACQUES-LOUIS DAVID — *Portrait of a Young Man*
65. ANTOINE-JEAN GROS — *Portrait of Prince Yusupov in Tatar Costume*
66. EUGÈNE DELACROIX — *After the Shipwreck*
67. CHARLES-FRANÇOIS DAUBIGNY — *Village on the Banks of the Oise*
68. VIRGILE-NARCISSE DIAZ DE LA PEÑA — *The Approaching Storm*

INTRODUCTION

The Pushkin State Museum of Fine Arts in Moscow, which celebrated its fiftieth anniversary in 1962, is one of the richest in the Soviet Union. Its collection of Western art, which includes many masterpieces, is second in Russia only to that of The Hermitage in Leningrad. Among the other art treasures of the Pushkin Museum are a collection of Faiyum portraits and Coptic woven fabrics; a valuable collection of prints from all nations and periods, including the largest collection of old Russian and Soviet prints in the U.S.S.R.; and one of the world's largest collections of plaster casts of great sculpture. In addition, the museum is an important center for the study of art history.

Fifty years, as museums go, is a relatively short time. Many museums, in Russia as elsewhere in the world, took centuries of effort to become what they are today, generally with the aid of generation after generation of private collectors. The history of the Pushkin Museum, however, followed a different pattern.

What might be called the ancestor of the Pushkin Museum was the so-called Munz-Kabinet, i.e., a collection of coins and medals, which was formed at the University of Moscow in the eighteenth century. The university also pioneered in certain types of museum work. It was among the Moscow professors that the idea of an "aesthetic museum" to serve educational purposes was conceived. The prototype of such an institution was the so-called Cabinet of Fine Arts created around 1850 for the benefit of students. Originally it contained only a small number of plaster casts and books on classical art. A few years later a chair of art history was founded. Gradually, as the advanced section of the Russian intelligentsia became aware of the social importance of art, the need began to be felt for expanding the Cabinet and transforming it into a public museum.

This project found its most eloquent champion in Professor I. I. Tsvetaev, a brilliant organizer and one of the most cultured men of his day. He is justly regarded as the founder of the present museum. He gained the support of prominent personalities and collected large sums of money among private individuals. The cornerstone of the museum was laid in 1898, and it was officially opened in 1912.

The building, one of Moscow's finest, was designed by the architect, R. I. Klein, who was inspired by the latest advances in the field of museum architecture. His work compares with the most modern museums of his day, both in Europe and in America. The museum's collections were inherited from the Cabinet, and most of the display rooms contained works used in the teaching of art history. Especially complete was the collection of plaster casts of Greek and Roman sculpture. Western European art from the early Middle Ages to the Renaissance was also represented by plaster casts, including the principal works of Michelangelo.

At first the museum had relatively few original works. Of these few, however, some were extremely valuable—a group of classical vases, excellent Egyptian objects collected by the well-known Egyptologist, V. S. Golenishchev, and thirteenth- and fourteenth-century Italian religious paintings.

A new epoch in the museum's history began with the October Revolution, which opened a vast field of possibilities for the development of culture and art in the Soviet Union. The museum's main task was now to make the treasures of art accessible to all the people. In the spring of 1920 an exhibition of projects for a Monument to the Emancipation of Labor was held in the museum, which had suffered damage during the revolution.

Now that all art collections were national property, museums could be organized according to new principles.

In the early 1920s the Pushkin Museum took steps to enlarge its collections, beginning with European painting. In 1923/24 it acquired the collections of the Tretiakov Gallery and the former Rumiantsev Museum, which included such masterpieces as Rembrandt's *Ahasuerus, Haman, and Esther;* Terborch's *Portrait of a Lady*; David's *Portrait of Ingres* (today known as *Portrait of a Young Man*); Corot's *Gust of Wind*; and works by Delacroix, Millet, Géricault, Courbet, and others.

In the late 1920s a number of important paintings were transferred from The Hermitage. They included *Rinaldo and Armida* and *Landscape with Hercules and Cacus* by Poussin; *Bivouac* by Watteau; *Portrait of the Artist's Brother* and *Portrait of an Old Woman* (sometimes called *Portrait of the Artist's Sister-in-Law*) by Rembrandt; *Bacchanal* and a number of sketches by Rubens; a *Madonna* by Cranach; *Satyr Visiting a Peasant* by Jordaens; *Flight into Egypt* by Murillo; and *David with Head of Goliath* by Feti. Among the works that had formerly belonged to private collectors we may mention *St. Sebastian* by Boltraffio; *The Rape of Europa* by Claude Lorrain; *Hercules and Omphale* by Boucher; a still life by Chardin; and *View of the Village of Egmont* by Jacob van Ruisdael.

In 1948 many works formerly in the Museum of Modern Western Art were transferred to the Pushkin Museum. These included the Shchukin and Morozov collections. Among the new acquisitions were *The Boulevard des Capucines* by Claude Monet; *Dancers in Blue* by Degas; *Nude* and *Portrait of Jeanne Samary* by Renoir; *The Banks of the Marne* by Cézanne; *After the Rain* and the *Prisoners' Round* by Van Gogh; *The Artist's Studio* and *Red Fishes* by Matisse; *Girl on a Ball* by Picasso; and a number of oils by Gauguin, Sisley, Pissarro, Bonnard, Marquet, and other artists.

With all these acquisitions the museum now owns one of the world's finest collections of seventeenth-century Dutch painting and of seventeenth- and eighteenth-century French painting. Its collection of nineteenth- and twentieth-century French paintings is outstanding for the variety and value of the works.

In 1924 the museum took over the Rumiantsev Museum's vast collection of prints, which served as the nucleus for the Pushkin Museum's Print Room, now including more than 300,000 items.

Between 1920 and 1930 the museum was enriched from new sources—archaeological excavations, exchanges with other museums, and purchases. The museum first organized archaeological excavations in 1926, on the northern shore of the Black Sea, and later in Transcaucasia. In this way the museum obtained more than 16,000 items, the best of which are exhibited in a gallery devoted to the art and culture of the cities on the northern coast of the Black Sea.

From the outset, the museum kept in close contact with living Soviet art, acquiring representative Soviet graphic works, and organizing the Soviet division of the Print Room. With the help of an official committee of experts, the museum has been able to supplement other divisions of its collection. In recent years it has acquired a bronze bust of Molière by Houdon, a study for the *Marseillaise* by Rude, two excellent paintings by Ostade, and *View of Venice*, the only work by Turner in the U.S.S.R.

A number of foreign artists have donated works to the museum out of sympathy with the Soviet Union. In 1920 the English painter, Frank Brangwyn, bequeathed it a complete collection of his etchings and lithographs. In 1960 the well-known American artist, Rockwell Kent, donated a complete set of his illustrated books, as well as twenty-six paintings and a number of manuscripts. Léger, Matisse, Diego Rivera, Renato Guttuso, and others have also given works to the museum.

As the museum kept on acquiring treasures of world art, its importance as a center of research in art history grew apace. The museum's scientific activities take many forms—monographs by individual authors and more general works involving collaboration, the preparation of catalogues and guidebooks, the attribution of works, etc. All these activities provide a solid basis for the pursuit of the museum's primary task, the education of the public.

Assimilation of the classical heritage is an essential element in the intellectual life of the Soviet population. Constant contact with the masterpieces of art is a prerequisite for harmonious personal development, and a means of spiritual enrichment and refinement of the individual's sensibility.

The museum's popularizing activities have yielded rich results. Muscovites from all walks of life are frequent visitors to the museum—as many as 800,000 per year. The museum's educational activities cover a vast range. First of all, it provides more than 5,000 guided tours every year. These include both general surveys and studies of particular collections. In addition, there are a considerable number of lectures—about 600 per year, either in the auditorium of the museum or outside, in Moscow and in other cities of the U.S.S.R.

An important part in the aesthetic education of the masses is played by the Universities for Popular Culture, which were created a few years ago. A University of Fine Arts, which gives two two-year courses, is attached to the museum. Attendance has been growing steadily. Students, factory workers, and white-collar workers are given a solid grounding in art history. Utilizing its highly qualified staff and special experience, the museum is able to participate actively in the work of other Popular Universities both in and outside Moscow.

The museum gives special attention to children. It maintains close contacts with schools and educational groups, and co-operates with teachers. The museum's school activities are closely tied in with the secondary-school curriculum, and visits to the museum are now obligatory in all Moscow schools.

Special lectures are provided for schoolchildren, covering art history, numismatics, archaeology, painting, sculpture, and drawing. In 1959 the Young Art Historians was founded, a club which has about 500 members consisting of pupils from the eighth to the eleventh grades. The club organizes lectures and seminars on foreign art. One of its aims is to encourage young people to help popularize art. The members prepare guided tours and organize exhibitions (of reproductions) in schools. In this manner children acquire respect for cultural and patriotic values.

During vacations the museum organizes special days, each dedicated to a specific theme—Young Archaeologist's Day, Young Painter's Day, Young Art Collector's Day, etc. The young people meet eminent art historians and artists, attend lectures, ask questions, and organize exhibitions of their own works.

13

The museum helps schools with their art collections and maintains close contact with secondary-school and university students. Nor does it neglect other groups of the population, organizing special days for collective farmers, soldiers, and factory workers. During the fifty-two years of its existence, the museum has held over 400 exhibitions, and thereby broad sections of the population have become familiar with its collections. One of the most important exhibitions of this type was the Rembrandt exhibition, held before the Second World War, when 254 original works by the great Dutch painter were shown. About half a million visitors came to this major cultural event during the four months it was open.

At present, the museum holds from ten to fourteen exhibitions a year, comprising works from both Soviet and foreign collections. We mention just a few of these to suggest the range of the museum's interests: works from the Dresden Museum (1955), Nineteenth-Century French Painting (1956), Chinese Painting (1957), English Painting (1960), Mexican Art (1960), Yugoslav Primitives (1961), Italian Gold and Silver (1962), Icelandic Painting (1963), as well as a number of one-man shows: Rembrandt, Menzel, Marquet, Matejko, Picasso, Kent, Guttuso, Léger, etc.

In addition, the museum organizes more than eighty traveling exhibits every year, both of original paintings and prints and of reproductions. Between four and five million people in various cities see these.

The art treasures of the museum are in great demand in foreign countries. In the course of recent years paintings have been sent on loan to exhibitions held in Rome, Paris, Venice, London, and other cities.

An important part in the museum's various activities is played by its auxiliary departments, such as the library and the workshops for restoring art objects. On two occasions the museum's expert restorers have faced real challenges. During the Second World War, the museum's treasures had to be evacuated and looked after under extremely unfavorable conditions. They passed this test with flying colors: not a single work was damaged

Then, after the war, the Pushkin Museum was asked by the government to look after the treasures of German museums liberated from the Nazis by the Red Army. Many works of art had been seriously damaged and were patiently restored between 1945 and 1955. In the end the Soviet government was able to return them in excellent condition to the German people.

In recent years the museum has broadened its international contacts. Exchanges of publications and art works, and the visits of prominent European, American, and Asian art historians to the museum have proved fruitful. Only a few years ago foreign specialists attributed to the famous Hermitage a number of masterpieces which were actually in the Pushkin Museum. Today errors of this type are scarcely possible. Experts from a number of countries have become familiar with the Pushkin Museum, and it is widely recognized as containing one of the most interesting collections of world art.

It is to be hoped that the present work will make the museum known to a still larger public.

The text of this work has been prepared by K. M. Malitskaya, curator of the museum's department of Western European Art, with the help of staff members including T. A. Borovaya, I. N. Golomshtok, K. S. Egorova, A. N. Zamyatina, I. A. Kuznetsova, D. S. Libman, O. D. Nikityuk, M. S. Senenko, and R. D. Shurinova.

I. ANTONOVA
Director of the Pushkin Museum

THE FAIYUM PORTRAITS

(Plates 1–7)

Some art historians have used the term "ancient Impressionism" in reference to these early portraits, because they are characterized by striking freedom of treatment. They were discovered accidentally in ancient graves located in the Faiyum oasis in Egypt. When they were first shown in Europe a number of experts doubted their authenticity: so perfect was the execution and so well-preserved the colors. But later excavations in the Faiyum disclosed hundreds more of the same type of work and confirmed that these tomb portraits were painted between the first and the fourth centuries A.D. Elements of Greek and Roman culture are combined with Egyptian influences in these admirable specimens of encaustic painting. The oldest of them, such as the *Portrait of a Man in a Blue Toga* (first or second century A.D.) and the *Portrait of a Dark-Skinned Woman* (second half of second century A.D.), were certainly done from nature. They were framed and kept at home. When the sitters died, their portraits were placed in the grave with their mummified remains, in the position of the head.

The works dating from the first and second centuries are faithful to the traditions of Hellenistic art. The figures are generally portrayed bust high, in three-quarter view, facing the beholder. But even though the pose never varies, the portraits are fully individualized, almost psychological in their penetration.

The *Portrait of a Middle-Aged Woman*, dating from the third century, reveals an entirely different approach. Although the head is turned a bit to one side, the portrait still seems rigidly frontal. The expressive drawing stresses the absence of depth. The medium employed is tempera, and it has been put on with a brush. The paint is applied very thinly and evenly, contours are rendered in unbroken lines, and the execution is rapid. The artist has aimed less at getting a likeness than at expressing the sitter's state of mind. The ascetic character of the work shows that at the time it was painted art had become subordinate to Christian ideology, which in this period was slowly supplanting the Hellenistic ideal of the good life.

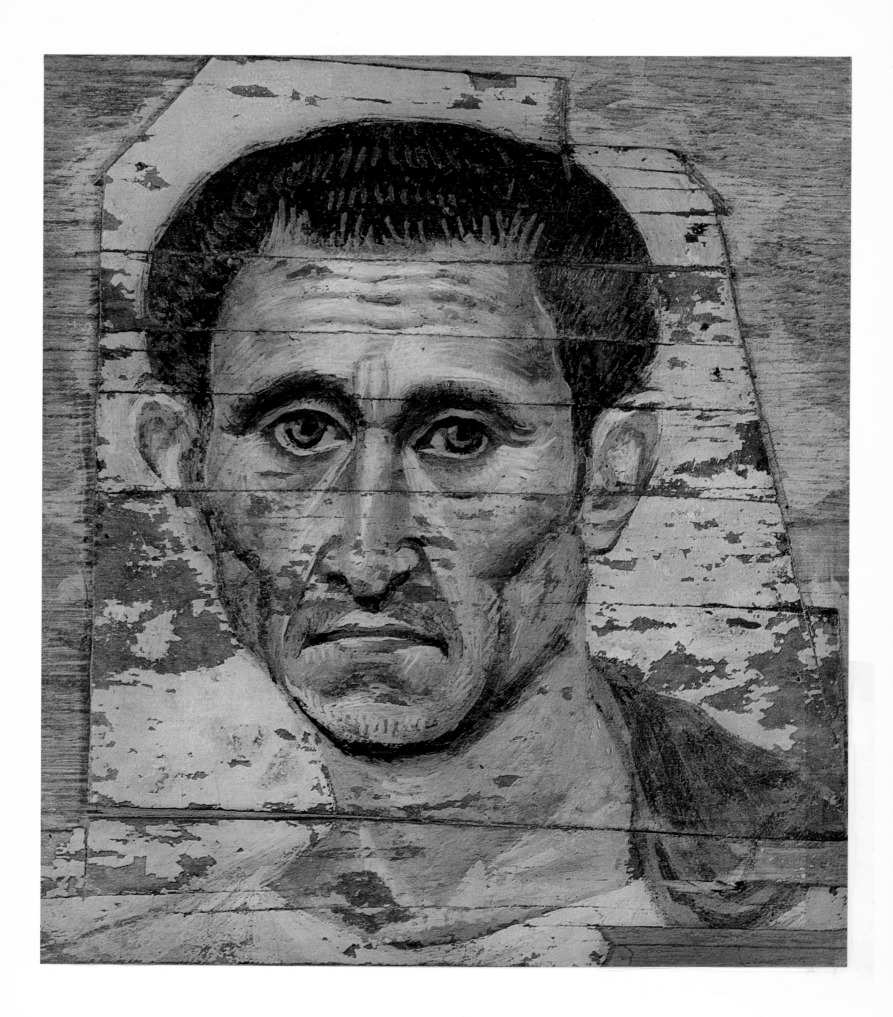

PLATE 2

FAIYUM PORTRAIT

Middle of 2nd century A.D.

Portrait of a Dark-Skinned Young Man

Encaustic on wood, $13\frac{3}{4} \times 8\frac{1}{4}''$
Formerly Collection Nechaev-Maltsev

PLATE 3

FAIYUM PORTRAIT

Middle of 2nd century A.D.

Portrait of a Middle-Aged Man

Encaustic and tempera on wood, $16\frac{3}{8} \times 7\frac{3}{4}''$
Formerly Collection V. S. Golenishchev

PLATE 4

FAIYUM PORTRAIT

Second half of 2nd century A.D.

Portrait of a Light-Skinned Man

Encaustic and tempera on wood, $15\frac{5}{8} \times 8\frac{1}{4}''$
Formerly Collection V. S. Golenishchev

PLATE 5

FAIYUM PORTRAIT

Middle of 2nd century A.D.

Portrait of a Dark-Skinned Man

Encaustic on wood, $15\frac{5}{8} \times 8\frac{1}{8}''$
Formerly Collection V. S. Golenishchev

BYZANTINE SCHOOL

PLATE 8

BYZANTINE MASTER

11th century

St. Pantheleimon

Encaustic on wood, 20½ × 13⅜″ · Formerly Tretyakov Gallery, Moscow

That this is a rare example of the classical style of the Macedonian dynasty is evident from the frontality of the figure, the severity of the face with the large eyes looking at the viewer, and the golden background. These are all characteristic of the elaborate iconography of the period, which aimed above all at spiritualization. The colors are applied thickly in clearly distinct areas: the himation is bright red and at the neck there is a glimpse of a green tunic bordered in brown that is worn underneath; the hands and face are pinkish-brown, with darker brown shadows that are the same color as the hair that frames the face. The halo is indicated by a circle of tiny dots over the gold ground. The saint's name is inscribed at the upper right and upper left.

The technique of encaustic painting had come down to the Byzantine masters from the ancient world.

PLATE 9

SCHOOL OF CONSTANTINOPLE

14th century

The Twelve Apostles

Tempera on wood, 15 × 13⅜″ · Formerly Historical Museum, Moscow

This icon is a precious example of Byzantine painting in the first half of the fourteenth century. In this period, which historians call "the Paleologue Renaissance," Byzantine art was losing the monumentality and rigidity of the earlier periods. It was becoming more refined, and a tendency to the pictorial and the dynamic was asserting itself. The forms were getting more graceful, the colors more delicate.

Although the arrangement is isocephalic, the attitudes and gestures of the apostles are free and easy, and the many small folds of drapery produce an effect of movement. The grayish-blue, greenish-brown, and grayish-lavender tones of the clothing are enhanced with whites. The subtly modeled faces are individually expressive. The ground the apostles are standing on is green. There is a gold background at the top; it is not especially brilliant, nor is the gold of the halos. Across the upper edge the Greek names of the apostles are written in vermilion.

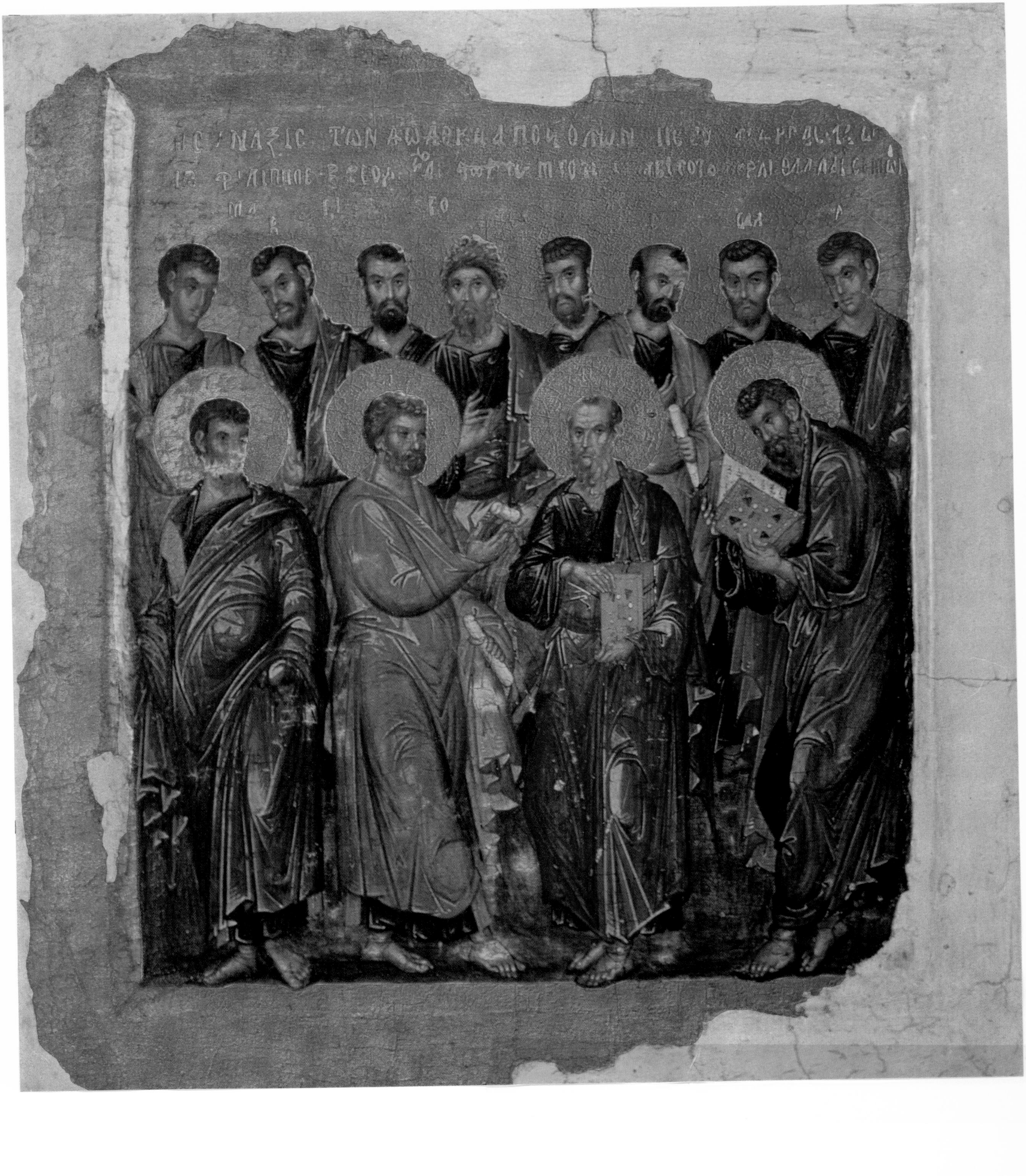

ITALIAN SCHOOL

PLATE 10

SCHOOL OF PISA

13th century

Virgin and Child

Tempera on wood, 68½ × 33⅛″ · Formerly Regional Museum, Smolensk

In the thirteenth century Byzantine influence was strong in Pisa, where a large group of Greek masters had settled after the capture of Constantinople by the Crusaders in 1204. At that time certain elements of Byzantine art were combined with Romanesque art, giving rise to a style known as the *maniera greca*.

Virgin and Child (shown seated on a throne) is a typical example of this style. Although the work is characterized by the monumentality of thirteenth-century Byzantine painting—the treatment is flat, and the folds of drapery rendered in golden lines are decorative—certain features betray its local origin. The delicately executed face is gentle and expresses simple human feeling—motherly tenderness; the cheeks are touched with pink. The Child is shown in a frontal pose, but the face is less stiffly rendered. The Virgin's halo is ornamented with a motif in relief, and that of the Child with a Greek cross.

PLATE I I

SEGNA DI BONAVENTURA

died c. 1331

Crucifixion

Tempera on wood, $85\frac{1}{4} \times 57\frac{1}{8}''$ · Formerly Collection Shchukin, Moscow

Unlike other works attributed to Segna di Bonaventura, this *Crucifixion* is signed and hence unquestionably authentic. However, there are serious disagreements over the date. Some experts believe this is an early work, executed before 1311, i.e., before the artist had seen works by Duccio, who became an important influence on Bonaventura, as we can see in his *Crucifixion* at Arezzo. In support of this view, it has been pointed out that the *Crucifixion* in the Pushkin Museum lacks the lyricism of this artist's later works and is distinguished rather by its monumentality, dramatic intensity, and general treatment. Other historians, however, adduce these very features as proof that the work dates from the artist's maturity, after he had freed himself from Duccio's influence and had achieved an original style. Be that as it may, this work shows the artist in full possession of his talent. The master displays relatively good knowledge of anatomy; he renders the intensity of Christ's suffering in the face and in the clenched hands. The execution is masterly, the colors are harmonious, and the subtle modeling brings out the structure of the body.

PLATE 12

SANDRO BOTTICELLI

1444/45–1510

The Virgin of the Annunciation

Tempera on wood, transferred to canvas; each section, $17\frac{3}{4} \times 5\frac{1}{8}''$
Formerly The Hermitage, Leningrad

This work, framed together with the figure of the archangel, is a section of an Annunciation scene for a small altarpiece. Two panels of the same height, with the figures of St. Jerome and St. Dominic (now in The Hermitage), may have belonged to the same altarpiece.

The altarpiece was painted in the 1490s, when the artist's clear, poetic vision of the world was disturbed by grave social upheavals in his native Florence. The banishment of the Medicis, in whose court Botticelli had worked from about 1470 on, and Savonarola's passionate sermons against the Pope and the Florentine patriciate deeply affected him. He renounced the mythological and literary subjects that he had treated in most of his earlier works. Haunted by a morbid religiosity, he plunged into a world of restless and exalted images. The Annunciation was usually treated in fifteenth-century Italian art as a joyful holiday; Botticelli interprets it as a highly dramatic event. Mary is shown frightened by the tidings the archangel brings her. Her face is distorted with grief, her eyes are lowered. The restless rhythm of the silhouette and drapery suggests nervous trembling. The narrow wing of the altarpiece seems to compress her within its boundaries, to prevent her from standing erect. The color scheme, based on cool gray-blues and lavenders, contributes to the over-all impression. The bright spots of vermilion (the book and the shoe) introduce shrill accents.

PLATE 13

PERUGINO

1446–1523

Virgin and Child

Oil on canvas, 20⅛ × 15″ · Formerly The Hermitage, Leningrad

Perugino became known primarily because of his famous pupil, Raphael. Recently, however, the question has been raised whether he was not influenced by the enchantingly harmonious art of the man so long regarded as his pupil. It is hard to believe that Perugino himself had worked under Andrea del Verrocchio in Florence, an artist characterized by precise, lively drawing and fond of vivid attitudes and movements. In any event, he never forgot the tender lyricism of the Umbrian landscape, with its delicate trees and gently sloping hills, such as can be seen behind the Virgin in this painting, who is portrayed in harmony with the over-all atmosphere of the work.

The Virgin's head is gently tilted; her long fingers touch the Child affectionately. She is a young Italian woman whose maternal love moves us, but she is permeated with a poetic melancholy that counteracts her earthliness. Nothing spoils the limpid harmony of the picture. The fluid contour lines that define the figure are continued in the landscape background where a soft evening light bathes the hills. The colors of the clothing are subdued, without bright spots. The atmosphere of the work and the figure of the Virgin bring to mind Raphael. The painting may date from the beginning of the sixteenth century.

A similar work is to be found in the Borghese Gallery in Rome.

PLATE 14

CIMA DA CONEGLIANO

c. 1459–1517/18

Virgin and Child

Oil on wood, transferred to canvas in 1872; 16½ × 13¾"
Formerly Collection E. V. Gabrichevsky

The *Virgin and Child* is one of Cima's favorite subjects. His gentle lyrical talent matured in the small provincial town of Conegliano, north of Venice, and the image of quiet love suited his temperament. His Madonnas are pensive young women who tenderly press the Child to them and look at the viewer with a trustful expression.

From 1492 on, Cima worked in Venice where he was influenced by the great Bellini. The work shown here was painted under this influence. Both the composition showing the Madonna against drapery and a landscape, and the motif of the child's feet placed one on the other are typical of Bellini. Like other Venetian painters of his day, Cima assigns an important place to nature, to man's environment. In his landscapes, which we occasionally recognize as views of Conegliano, he seeks to paint a nature attuned to man's inner life. In this work, the Madonna's gentle calm is echoed by the distant mountains in the golden light of sunset.

The color scheme is typical of the Venetian School. The saturated winy reds and dark greens of the clothing, and the green of the drapery are unified by the same golden glow.

PLATE 15

DOSSO DOSSI

1479–1542

Landscape in the Thebaid with Scenes from the Lives of the Saints

Oil on canvas, 26¾ × 34¼″
Formerly Museum of History of Religion, Moscow

This landscape is very unusual for Italian Renaissance art, which is strongly anthropocentric. But despite the presence of the little figures of saints—St. Francis receiving the stigmata, St. Jerome with the Cross, St. Catherine, St. Christopher with the Child Jesus on his back, St. George battling with the dragon—the work was primarily intended as a view of nature and is, in fact, one of the earliest landscapes in the history of Italian painting.

Nature as painted by Dossi is fantastic. It is not a specific site; the artist freely interprets his conception of the world around him, which the men of the Renaissance at that time were rediscovering for themselves. The artist does not dwell on details, he opens a broad panorama for the viewer. The steep mountains covered with vegetation, the plain enveloped in a gray-blue mist, the foaming waterfall, the blue lake, the light-blue sky and the dark-blue storm cloud, the water mill, the inaccessible castle—all these merge into a single world, still little explored, but full of poetic charm and seductive in its unknown riches.

The composition seems to include several points of view. The compact scene at the left contrasts with the vista opening into depth at the right, which is constructed in accordance with the laws of linear and aerial perspective. Three planes are clearly distinguished: the foreground in brown, the middle ground in green, and the background in misty blues.

A similar interest in landscape is found in the Italy of that time only in the art of the great Venetians, Giorgione and Titian.

PLATE 16

AGNOLO BRONZINO

1503–72

The Holy Family

Tempera on wood, transferred to canvas in 1857; 46⅛ × 39"
Formerly State Museum of Antiquities, Moscow

Agnolo Bronzino was twenty-four when the Spanish troops sacked Rome in 1527. To contemporaries this event spelled the end of the Renaissance. Italy underwent a deep social and spiritual crisis. Free cities, the cradles of Renaissance culture, came under monarchic rule. In 1530 the republic of Florence fell after a heroic resistance. The same year, Bronzino was appointed court painter to Cosimo Medici, Duke of Tuscany. He became one of the central figures of Mannerism—the official courtly style of sixteenth-century Italy. Celebrated for his portraits, he also painted religious works, such as the one shown here.

Particularly impressive in this work is its masterful composition, which fully embodies what the Mannerists considered the most valuable element in a work of art—the so-called *invenzione*. The four figures—Mary, Joseph, Jesus, and John the Baptist—form a unity that has been achieved by the rhythm of deliberately complicated movements and the play of overlapping lines. Despite this formal unity, the artist does not succeed in surmounting the coldness and mutual isolation of the figures. Cold grandeur, impassivity, and pride—features of the aristocratic ideal—dominate the characterization of the figures.

Bronzino treated the same subject in several other works. This painting is the latest (it dates from between 1555 and 1560) and apparently the best. It is very possibly the work that, according to Giorgio Vasari, was painted by Bronzino for one Carlo Gerardi in Pistoia.

PLATE 17

PAOLO VERONESE

1528–88

Minerva

Oil on canvas, 11 × 6¼″ · Formerly The Hermitage, Leningrad

Just as a pearl mysteriously reflects the colors of sky and sea, so this little *Minerva*—almost a monochrome study—discloses the artistic riches of the great Venetian painter, Paolo Veronese.

Leaning on a spear, Minerva in a transparent, golden tunic stands in a semicircular niche. Elusive green reflections glide everywhere, gathering in the green cloak which is tied in a knot at the goddess' waist and in the shadow she casts on the wall. The over-all silvery tone absorbs the golden sheen of the helmet and the shield with the image of Medusa's head, and the olive greens of the wall and the fabric, resulting in the extraordinary complex color harmonies that the Russian painter V. I. Surikov called "the tones of the Adriatic in Veronese's works."

The present study was probably a preliminary sketch for a mural in a suburban villa, the decoration of which Veronese worked on from the early 1550s to about 1565. At that time many prominent Venetians built summer residences in the sub-Alpine countryside. Here they sought peace and relaxation in the pleasures of rural life. These villas were generally simple and cozy, very unlike the Venetian palaces; many were designed by the great Palladio. The murals in these villas most often represented mythological subjects. Veronese's poetic interpretation of them shows how deeply ancient culture influenced the men of the Renaissance. A companion piece to this work, entitled *Diana*, is in The Hermitage.

PLATE 18

BERNARDO STROZZI

1581–1644

Aging Beauty

Oil on canvas, 53⅛ × 42⅞″ · Formerly Rumiantsev Museum, Moscow

The art of Strozzi is associated with two northern Italian cities, Genoa and Venice, both of which remained faithful to the realist tradition throughout the seventeenth century. Strozzi was brought up on the best models of sixteenth century Venetian painting; but he was also influenced by his contemporary Caravaggio and by Rubens, the great Flemish painter. As a rule, Strozzi's canvases are of large format, with large figures in the foreground. When treating a genre scene, he never reduces it to detailed description, to mere anecdote; he always aims at deeper meaning, on a well-nigh monumental scale. In this work old age and ugliness are not meant to be ridiculed; they are shown rather as the inevitable fate of all living creatures. The composition rests on a number of contrasts—between the bright ribbon and the soft texture of the velvet on the one hand, and the coarse flabby skin of the old woman on the other; between the gracefulness of the rose and the stiffness of the fingers holding it; between the sparkle of the pearls and the wrinkles of the neck; between the downiness of the feather and the sparse gray hair. These contrasts are sharper and more convincing than the more obvious one between the homely faces of the young servant girls and their mistress' aged, but original and expressive, face.

Because of its intense colors, vigorous modeling, and accurate rendering of textures, *Aging Beauty* is one of Strozzi's finest works. It probably dates from the artist's Venetian period, which began in 1630.

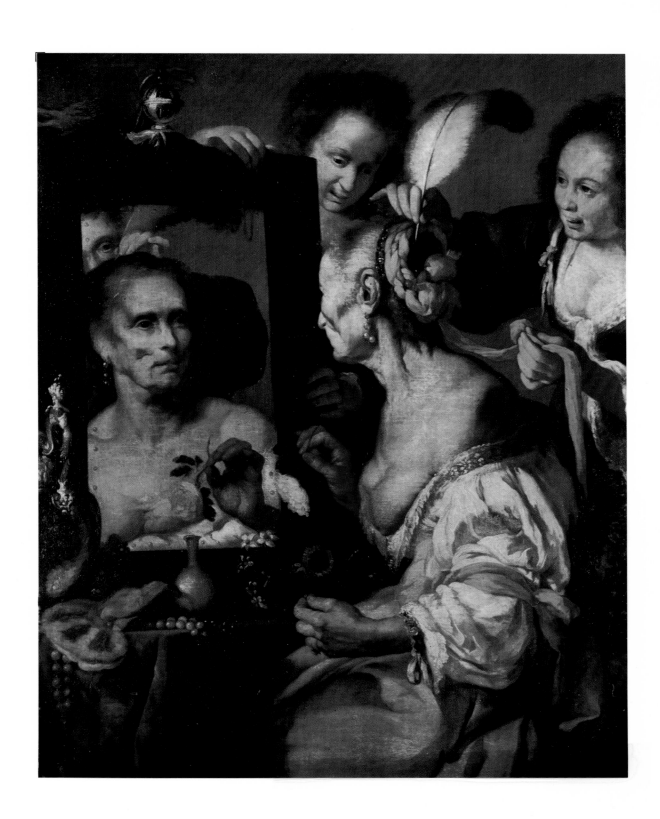

PLATE 19

SALVATOR ROSA

1615–73

Soldiers Playing Dice

Oil on canvas, $31\frac{7}{8} \times 25\frac{1}{4}''$
Formerly The Hermitage, Leningrad

Salvator Rosa, painter, engraver, and poet, belongs to the School of Naples, where he studied under Ribera. He traveled a great deal and stayed for some time in Florence and in Rome. He never adopted the grand style of the Baroque masters. Like Feti and Magnasco, he was a rebel, keeping off the beaten track of official art.

All three artists painted hermits and tramps and composed landscapes that are distinctly romantic in character. Rosa's works include mysterious, gloomy landscapes with battle scenes, and figures with austere, virile faces, some of which are self-portraits. This painting, too, with its nocturnal landscape and the light-flecked armor of the soldiers, is pervaded by a romantic atmosphere.

A similar painting is to be found in the Dulviccio Gallery.

PLATE 20

DOMENICO FETI

1589–1623

David with Head of Goliath

Oil on canvas, $41\frac{3}{8} \times 31\frac{7}{8}''$
Formerly The Hermitage, Leningrad

This painting has an interesting history. It traveled the long way from the collection of Charles I of England to the Pushkin Museum in Moscow, passing through the collections of M. Crozat and Abbé Lemoine. In the museum in Besançon there is a painting attributed to Grimm, which is obviously a copy of Feti's work.

Authentic heir to the great Venetian painters of the Renaissance, Feti was also influenced by Caravaggio and Rubens. His small poetic paintings, often inspired by Biblical parables, reflect a genuine feeling for the beauty of real life. It is all the more surprising, then, to find him treating so heroic a subject as David and Goliath, which was often treated during the Renaissance. Feti's David is no Renaissance hero, however, but a courtier with exquisite manners. His features are so individual that we may be dealing with a portrait. The painting is done in a scale of dark browns—in this respect, too, it is an exception among his works.

PLATE 21

ALESSANDRO MAGNASCO

1667–1749

Training the Magpie

Oil on canvas, 15¾ × 11¾″ · Formerly State Museum Reserves, Moscow

Magnasco departs from the Genoese tradition of genre painting, and shows no enthusiasm for Caravaggio or the Flemish artists. His canvases, which are painted in a monochrome scale of cool tones, occasionally enhanced by unexpected bright accents, are notable for their emotionalism, nervous intensity, and romantic mood. His energetic, nervous brush strokes communicate a special vibrancy.

This work illustrates his style admirably. Against the background of a dilapidated landscape, a tramp—one of the artist's favorite subjects—is trying to train a magpie. The restless atmosphere of this work is a long way from the usual genre painting.

Magnasco had a considerable influence on a group of Venetian artists, among them Francesco Guardi.

PLATE 22

GIOVANNI BATTISTA TIEPOLO

1696–1770

The Death of Dido

Oil on canvas, $15\frac{3}{4} \times 24\frac{3}{4}''$ · Formerly The Hermitage, Leningrad

According to legend, Dido was the daughter of the emperor of Tyre and founded Carthage; Vergil celebrated her in the *Aeneid*. Deserted by her beloved Aeneas, she voluntarily mounted the funeral pyre. This small sketch by Tiepolo is an authentic masterpiece. Painted *alla prima* with the subtlest nuances, it has preserved for us the great Venetian master's vitality and vibrant palette. The monumental character of the composition seems to support the conjecture that the sketch was a preliminary study for a large fresco—that was never executed—destined for the Vergil room in the Villa Valmarano. The sketch may date from 1757; by then Tiepolo had attained full maturity and was a master of decorative mural painting.

Tiepolo, to whom eighteenth-century Venice owes much of its fame, spent the last years of his life in Madrid; his brilliant art influenced Goya.

PLATE 23

CANALETTO (ANTONIO CANALE)

1697–1768

The Betrothal of the Doge and the Adriatic

Oil on canvas, 71⅝ × 101⅞″ · Formerly The Hermitage, Leningrad

Canaletto is one of the most famous masters of eighteenth-century Venice. In this painting, which depicts the traditional celebration of the marriage between the Doge and the Adriatic Sea, we see Venice in all its splendor, with its admirable palaces and unique piazzas. The Doge is shown throwing a golden ring into the sea: according to legend, this offering propitiated the sea and made her friendly to Venetian sailors. The Doge's gold-and-red ship—the *Bucentaur*—is just off the center of the city: we see the Palace of the Doges, the church of San Marco, and the old Sansovino library. On the Grand Canal, gondolas filled with elegant Venetians have gathered. The graphic clarity of the silhouettes and bright spots of color harmonize with the well-rendered sunlight, which brings out the solemn splendor of the scene.

A companion piece, *The Reception of the French Ambassador in Venice*, is in The Hermitage.

PLATE 24

PIETRO LONGHI

1702–85

Lobby of a Gambling House

Oil on canvas, 28 × 21¼″ · Formerly Collection Benediktov, Moscow

The Ridotto casino was a center of life in eighteenth-century Venice. It was frequented by rich patricians and prominent foreigners. They came not only to gamble but also to discuss new plays, organize parties and masked balls, and engage in amorous and political intrigues.

Goldoni, a close friend of Longhi, left an excellent description of the Ridotto in his memoirs. Longhi was at his best in genre subjects, and he has given us a whole chronicle of Venetian life in his day. The painting in the Pushkin Museum is exceptional among his works for its great pictorial qualities. Most of his other canvases are drabber in color and more monotonous in treatment.

PLATE 25

FRANCESCO GUARDI

1712–93

Alexander Views the Body of Darius

Oil on canvas, 37⅜ × 49⅝" · Formerly Rumiantsev Museum, Moscow

With Giovanni Battista Tiepolo, Guardi is one of the most brilliant representatives of eighteenth-century European painting, and the significance of his work is not confined to Venice. He made his debut in the workshop of his older brother, Giovanni Antonio, and recently art historians have been concerned with the attribution of canvases dated from the period of their collaboration. In addition to mythological and religious paintings, their workshop executed a large number of copies of sixteenth- and seventeenth-century masterpieces.

Alexander Views the Body of Darius is most likely such a copy. The original, a work by Langetti, a seventeenth-century painter, has been published by the Italian historian, Bonzi, under the title, *Priam Asking Achilles for the Body of Hector*. Although this work is a copy, its great merits as a work by the renowned Venetian can readily be seen. Because of its romantic emotion and violence, masterful execution, and intense colors, this canvas is one of Guardi's finest. The translucent landscape in the background anticipates the later manner of the artist, who was to become famous for his Venetian views. He probably executed this work around 1750 when he was painting in his brother's workshop. What had been intended as a copy turned out to be a masterpiece in its own right.

PLATE 26

FRANCESCO GUARDI

1712-93

View of a Venetian Courtyard

Oil on canvas, 15 × 10¼″ · Formerly Collection Shchukin, Moscow

Francesco Guardi is the poet of Venice. He is less attracted by sumptuous palaces than by ordinary corners of the city, which other painters generally scorned. The light, the air, the shimmering sunshine, and a few touches of bright color transfigure everyday objects, communicating to Guardi's views a special subtlety, a kind of spirituality. Unlike his contemporary Canaletto, Guardi does not "portray" one or another city scene, but freely rearranges architectural motifs that have caught his eye. And without altering external appearances, he creates arbitrary spatial relationships.

This painting is a companion piece to another view of Venice, also in the Pushkin Museum.

SPANISH SCHOOL

PLATE 27

JUSEPE DE RIBERA

1591–1652

St. Anthony the Anchorite

Oil on canvas, 29⅞ × 25¼″ · Formerly Rumiantsev Museum, Moscow

Ribera was one of the most prominent painters of the first half of the seventeenth century. His work has rare pictorial merits: powerful chiaroscuros and firm, bold brush strokes are accurately combined to render nature with intensely expressive vigor. Ribera often took his models from among the poorest classes of Naples, where he spent almost all his life. To attractive young faces he preferred the faces of persons on whom long experience of life had left its imprint. He often gave his models the names of saints.

The figure shown here represents St. Anthony, as is indicated by the blue cross, in the form of a tau, painted on the dark clothes.

Two bright accents—the face and the hand—stand out against the graduated blues and grays that dominate the painting. Particularly felicitous is the rendering of the old man's face: the forehead furrowed with deep wrinkles, the eyes growing dim, the reddened eyelids, the white hair that frames the head.

Ribera used the same model for his St. Andrew (in the Prado), also dated 1647.

PLATE 28

FRANCISCO DE ZURBARÁN

1598–1664

The Christic Child

Oil on wood, 16½ × 18½″ · Formerly Collection Shuvalova, Leningrad

Zurbarán was one of the painters whose works helped the Spanish School to achieve a prominent place in seventeenth-century European art.

He is best known for religious works in which he portrayed eminent members of the monastic orders. He also painted children, who served him as models for scenes treating the childhood of Christ and Mary. In these works he displayed tender lyricism and genuine feeling.

The work shown here is a perfect example of his style. The Christ is admirable for spontaneity and directness. The colors applied in broad patches to form large serene areas give him a monumental character. The scale of tones is limited, but by boldly combining an intense blue with a straw yellow, by permeating the painting with light, and by elaborating the play of lights and shadows, Zurbarán achieves an effect of lightness. On the back of the canvas a phoenix has been engraved on a golden ground—a symbol of eternal rebirth.

This painting, executed by Zurbarán in the late 1630s, was part of an altarpiece in the Trinitarian Church in Seville, which was dedicated to St. Joseph.

PLATE 29

BARTOLOMÉ ESTEBAN MURILLO

1617–82

The Fruit Seller

Oil on canvas, 29⅞ × 24″ · Formerly The Hermitage, Leningrad

Murillo, who is closely associated with the realistic traditions of the School of Seville, was fond of everyday scenes. He painted the poor children of his native city and young peasants from the neighboring villages. The girl shown here is bringing fruit from the country to sell in town, carrying her basket with a shy smile and holding her kerchief to her face. The variegated colors and somewhat ponderous brush strokes, so different from the lightness that characterizes the artist's later work, suggest that this picture should be dated around 1650, that is, in Murillo's earliest phase.

A companion piece to this work, *Child with Dog*, is in The Hermitage.

PLATE 30

ANTONIO PEREDA THE ELDER

c. 1641–78

Still Life

Oil on canvas, 30¾ × 35⅞″ · Formerly The Hermitage, Leningrad

Antonio Pereda, one of the finest still-life painters of the School of Madrid in the sixteenth century, excels in rendering forms and textures. In the painting shown here we see a great variety of objects; an effect of unity is achieved by the predominance of red tones—the reds of the curtain and the vases, the reddish tinges in the sea shells.

The Hermitage owns another still life by Pereda that is looked upon as a companion piece to this painting, which is dated 1652.

PLATE 31

FRANCISCO JOSÉ DE GOYA

1746–1828

Dead Nun

Oil on canvas, mounted on wood; 11 × 16½″
Formerly Collection Ostroukhov, Moscow

This tiny canvas, almost a sketch, strikes us by the boldness with which the artist treated his subject. Particularly realistic is the deathly pale face of the young nun with its delicate features. The transparency of the skin is rendered in a palette of subtly shaded whites and grays. The head rests on a reddish-brown pillow, whose color blends harmoniously with the whites and blacks of the clothing and the gray background.

The freedom of execution and originality of technique are also noteworthy: it seems that the artist chiefly used a broad brush and in some places applied the paint with his fingers. The paint is so thin in some areas that the canvas can be seen through it; other areas are thickly covered. This technique suggests that the work belongs to the period of Goya's maturity. A comparison with the *Portrait of a Young Nun*, dated 1827, which was listed in the catalogue of the Bourbon-Bourbon Collection in Madrid in 1928, confirms this conjecture. We may conclude that the painting shown here is one of Goya's last works; it was doubtlessly executed in 1828, only a short time before his death.

GERMAN SCHOOL

PLATE 32

LUCAS CRANACH THE ELDER

1472–1553

Virgin and Child

Oil on wood, 22⅞ × 18⅛″ · Formerly The Hermitage, Leningrad

The work of Lucas Cranach the Elder falls within the period of the flowering of German art. Court painter to the Saxon Electors, he was one of the most prominent supporters of Luther and Melanchthon. His fondness for refined and delicate forms, which reflects an aristocratic ideal of art, is combined with a deep love for nature as he observed it in his native land and with his interest in the humanistic, philosophical, and moral problems of his epoch.

The work shown here is an admirable example of Cranach's art. As in most northern painters, lyricism is predominant. The landscape is an important element of the composition—the real-life environment of the figures. The massive mountains, the rivers, and the forest bathed in gentle light make the scene a vast image of the world, as limpid and serene as the Madonna's face, as pure as the Child's eyes. The depth of the maternal feeling and the harmony between man and nature expressed in this work endow the subject with profoundly human, poetic meaning.

PLATE 33

THE MASTER OF MESSKIRCH

16th century

Calvary

Oil on wood, 16½ × 23¼″ · Formerly Collection Shermetiev

This is one of the rare extant works by the German painter known only as the Master of Messkirch. The coats-of-arms shown in it are those of Rudolph von Ehingen (d. 1529) and his wife Sophie von Neuneck (d. 1539). The painting was certainly commemorative and was executed in the 1530s, after the death of Rudolph von Ehingen, but in his widow's lifetime.

The remarkably refined portrayal of Christ on the cross is a copy of a Dürer engraving, but the painter surrounded it with more primitive figures of his own invention. To the left are Mary and John; the German inscription on the scroll above them reproduces the words Christ addressed to them. The inscription to the right mentions the Roman centurion who was converted to belief in Christ as he watched the Crucifixion. The centurion is shown standing next to a sumptuously dressed, though somewhat comical, squire. Above these two figures are the coats-of-arms of Ehingen and Neuneck.

NETHERLANDISH SCHOOL

PLATE 34

MABUSE (JAN GOSSAERT)

c. 1478–c. 1536

Portrait of a Man

Oil on wood, $14\frac{1}{8} \times 11''$ · Formerly Collection Shuvalova, Leningrad

Jan Gossaert, called Mabuse after the name of his native town, is one of the greatest sixteenth-century Dutch painters. His religious and mythological compositions disclose the influence of Italian models, but in his portraits he continues and develops the great tradition of the fifteenth-century Dutch portraitists.

The Dutch School is represented in the Pushkin Museum by only a few works; this portrait painted on a dark ground, which re-creates the typical Dutch burgher of the period, is one of the finest of these. We do not know who the sitter was; a portrait of the same man, at a more advanced age, is in the Pratt Collection in New York.

PLATE 35

UNKNOWN DUTCH MASTER

Late 15th century

Portrait of Duchess Anne de Clèves

Oil on canvas, 12⅝ × 8⅞″ · Formerly Collection Leuchtenberg, Leningrad

The young woman represented is Anne of Burgundy, who in 1488 married Duke Antoine de Clèves. Her dress of extraordinary colors is extremely simple: her calm pose is unusually natural for princely portraits of that period. The face is not beautiful; the calm, concentrated expression speaks in favor of the conjecture suggested by the Latin inscription which celebrates the Nativity, namely, that this portrait was part of a diptych on a religious subject. The young woman absorbed in meditation seems to be gazing at some religious scene perhaps represented on the missing panel.

The simplicity and expressiveness of the pose, and the originality of the youthful face whose features, for all their individuality, bring to mind a definite type, suggest that the artist was a disciple of Geertgen, the great fifteenth-century Dutch painter who lived and worked at the St. John monastery in Haarlem.

PLATE 36

PIETER PIETERS

1540–1603

Woman Selling Fish

Oil on canvas, 44⅛ × 33⅛″ · Formerly The Hermitage, Leningrad

Pieter Pieters was one of a veritable dynasty of painters. Eldest son and pupil of Pieter Aertsen, who created the peasant genre in Dutch painting, he was the father of Pieter Pieters the Younger, one of the founders of the seventeenth-century Dutch School.

The work shown here admirably illustrates the school of Dutch genre painting initiated by Pieter Aertsen. The attractive young woman is looking at the viewer with a faint smile. But the painter seems particularly fascinated by the beauty of things. The wicker basket, the wood of the table, the red earthenware plate, the slippery wet bodies of the variously sized fishes, silvery with brown markings, all are rendered with great mastery.

Aertsen and his disciples (including his son Pieter Pieters) played an important part in the development of the Dutch still life, which reached a brilliant flowering in Holland and Flanders in the seventeenth century.

FLEMISH SCHOOL

PLATE 37

PETER PAUL RUBENS

1577–1640

Mucius Scaevola

Oil on wood, 16⅛ × 13¾" · Formerly Rumiantsev Museum, Moscow

Recently Rubens' sketches have been arousing increasing interest, as a number of publications and exhibitions attest. These works are appreciated as immediate expressions of the painter's personality, temperament, and brilliant mastery.

This oil study, which shows Scaevola putting his hand in the fire to prove his courage to the terrified enemy, is one of the most interesting. Despite the small format, it conveys a sense of the monumental. Unfortunately, the painting Rubens composed on this subject was destroyed during a fire in the Alcazar in Madrid in 1734. Only Van Dyck's copy of it has come down to us; it is in the Budapest Museum.

PLATE 38

PETER PAUL RUBENS

1577–1640

Study for a Triumphal Arch

Oil on wood, 26¾ × 27⅝″ · Formerly The Hermitage, Leningrad

Projects for temporary structures, such as those to be erected in 1645 on the occasion of the solemn entry of Prince Ferdinand into Antwerp, occupy a special place among Rubens' sketches and engravings. A number of these sketches are in The Hermitage.

Rubens' inexhaustible plastic imagination combines sculpture and painting with sumptuous architectural forms. In the central panel we see the prince taking leave of his father, Philip IV, king of Spain, then ruler of Flanders. Statues of ancient divinities personify Wisdom, Prosperity, and Victory. In the cloud of the central panel we see Duchess Isabella, who had died shortly before. Rubens here combines realistic and fantastic elements, as he does in the series on the life of Maria de Medici in The Louvre, and in many other works.

PLATE 39

FRANS SNYDERS

1579–1657

Still Life with Swan

Oil on canvas, 63¾ × 89¾″ · Formerly The Hermitage, Leningrad

Still life was one of the great Flemish master's favorite types of composition. Snyders was showered with commissions to paint immense decorative canvases like this one, which were hung in the dining rooms of Antwerp merchants and bankers, and in the refectories of wealthy monasteries.

When Snyders painted large tables piled up with all sorts of victuals, he celebrated the abundance of nature, whose rich gifts are destined to delight man. He chose the most expensive, most exquisite foods—the most luscious fruits, freshly killed game, lobsters, oysters, etc. The artist's father owned a well-known tavern in Antwerp, and so he had grown up amidst this culinary abundance.

The textures of the objects represented are beautifully rendered. We can almost feel the soft fur of the roebuck, the dog's thick coat, the boar bristles, the down of the swan and its firm wing feathers, the ripeness of the yellow pears, and the transparency of the grapes.

Nature's gifts, as Snyders represented them, delight the eye with their beautiful forms and colors. The snow-white swan stands out against the raspberry-red tablecloth, the motley plumage of the game birds, the deer's coat. The scarlet lobster on the embossed plate, the green squash, and the attractively arranged fruits in the basket compose a brilliant chromatic symphony. In celebrating the sensual pleasures of earthly life Snyders comes close to Rubens, in whose workshop he painted for many years, executing the flowers, fruits, and animals in the master's paintings.

The freedom of execution shown in this work suggests that it belongs to Snyders' mature period.

PLATE 40

ANTHONY VAN DYCK

1599–1641

Portrait of Adriaen Steevens' Wife

Oil on canvas, 44⅛ × 35⅞″ · Formerly The Hermitage, Leningrad

The inscription on the painting gives the date the work was completed, as well as the age of Mrs. Steevens: sixty-three. Judging by the coat-of-arms, her maiden name was Boschart. Another portrait, companion piece to this one, is also in the Pushkin Museum. It represents Adriaen Steevens, deputy mayor of Antwerp.

Van Dyck, the most talented of Rubens' pupils, left his native city at an early date, for while his master was there, his own role necessarily had to be a subordinate one. After several years in Italy he came back to Antwerp, renowned as a portraitist. Before leaving again, this time for England, he composed a series of remarkably accurate portraits, at once simple and delicate, to which the illustration shown here belongs.

PLATE 41

DAVID TENIERS THE YOUNGER

1610–90

Monkeys Playing Cards

Oil on wood, 9 × 11¾″ · Formerly Private Collection, Moscow

Today it is difficult to imagine the vogue David Teniers enjoyed all over Europe. His paintings, usually quite small and executed in attractive color, represent tipsy peasants and soldiers, scholars and alchemists, prosaic burghers, and devils and witches trying to seduce St. Anthony. These amusing subjects aroused widespread enthusiasm.

Occasionally, as in the work shown here, Teniers replaced the human figures with monkeys; like human beings, these animals carry swords, wear plumed hats, drink wine, and play cards. Teniers' scenes are comical, but not satirical. The viewer laughs at the monkeys, not at the people they are imitating.

DUTCH SCHOOL

PLATE 42

HENDRICK VAN AVERCAMP

1585–1634

Skaters

Oil on wood, 9½ × 15″ · Formerly Collection Shchukin, Moscow

Hendrick van Avercamp, one of the most attractive figures in Dutch painting, was a mute. He spent almost his entire life in his native town of Kampen and painted a large number of small-sized landscapes, executed with meticulous care.

Avercamp's favorite subject was the canals in winter, frozen over and filled with people. He produced countless pencil and watercolor sketches of rich burghers shown skating or playing hockey, children darting around over the ice, and poor people carrying bundles of firewood. In such landscapes, the artist scatters figures and groups, so as to combine genre scenes. In the painting shown, for instance, the foreground group with a lady whose skates are being fastened by her escort is a picture in itself.

Avercamp often made use of the same compositional plan. In this painting there are boats frozen in the ice at the left, and at the right the walls and towers of a fortress (perhaps of Kampen). The same elements turn up in one of his paintings owned by the Edinburgh Gallery.

Despite such repetitiveness, Avercamp's works charm us, probably owing to the painter's particularly attentive vision, and the care with which he recreates the gray surface of the ice and the soft blue mist in the background, as well as the pink tones of the walls and the varicolored clothes of the skaters. Airily light, rich in color, his painting has a jewel-like quality, describing the joys and travails of winter with verve and simplicity.

PLATE 43

WILLEM CLAESZ. HEDA

1594–1680/82

Still Life with Ham and Silver

Oil on wood, 38⅛ × 31½" · Formerly State Museum Reserves, Moscow

Willem Claesz. Heda, one of the great masters of the still life, was prominent among the painters of his native Haarlem and had many pupils. In the course of his long life he developed and perfected the principles of tonal painting, achieving a peak of virtuosity.

This work, a variation on the artist's "Breakfast" theme, is a brilliant example of his mature period. The light olive-gray background and the choice of objects are characteristic of his style. The silver pitcher, vase, mug, and plate give the artist opportunities for rendering the play of light on this metal. The white napkin and the red-pink ham, together with the various shades of gray in the rest of the painting, create refined color combinations. Every detail is rendered with the utmost accuracy, the forms true to life almost to the point of seeming real. As is often the case with Dutch landscape painters of the period, the colors are slightly subdued, and the whole is bathed in an almost imperceptible play of light that lends unity to the composition. The painting is signed and dated 1649.

PLATE 44

JAN VAN GOYEN

1596–1656

The River Waal Near Niemegen

Oil on canvas, 15¾ × 24¾″ · Formerly Collection Shchukin, Moscow

Jan van Goyen is justly regarded as the leading realist landscapist in Holland in the first half of the seventeenth century. Very active, endowed with great capacity for work, he left behind a large number of paintings and drawings representing Dutch villages, towns, roads, and rivers. His mature works, executed after he broke away from the picturesqueness and conventionalism of his first phase, are characterized by natural perspective and pictorial unity. He filled sketchbooks with drawings from nature, and later, in his oils, sought to render the essential features of each landscape, though he occasionally altered details and distances.

He painted the fortress of Waalhof near Niemegen on several occasions: he was particularly fond of this skyline of walls and towers, viewed from across the Waal. Signed and dated 1642, this picture belongs to his last period. By this time Van Goyen had gained deep insight into the connections between every element in the fluid atmosphere of a landscape. The calm waters of the Waal, the broad, overcast sky, the slightly blurred outlines of buildings and trees—everything seems bathed in a gray-brown mist, blended in a changing, uncertain light. A few touches of lighter color convey a feeling of movement going on within nature itself. The pictorial harmony poetically transfigures the usual Dutch landscape.

PLATE 45

SALOMON VAN RUYSDAEL

1600–70

Landscape with River

Oil on wood, 12¼″ × 19¼″ · Formerly Rumiantsev Museum, Moscow

Toward 1630 the Dutch realist landscape was acquiring its definitive form. Its most illustrious representative, besides Jan van Goyen, was Salomon van Ruysdael, who lived and worked in Haarlem. His sure, even mastery earned him great popularity both in his lifetime and after his death.

This small-size work of 1631 is typical of Dutch landscape painting in the first third of the seventeenth century. The river moving downstream and the diagonal line of the bank that emphasizes perspective define a compositional pattern to be found with many variations in Ruysdael and other Dutch painters.

In the 1630s Ruysdael worked in an almost monochromatic scale and rendered the atmosphere as a misty veil enveloping all objects. This artist's manner is distinguished by a tempered taste for detail and by a precision of color more marked than in Van Goyen. Ruysdael lovingly paints clumps of trees with foliage the color of a faded emerald; he captures the blue shimmer of water and the light made diffuse by the humid climate. The beauty of the Dutch landscape, simple to the point of austerity, seems to live again in his works.

PLATE 46

PIETER CODDE

1599–1678

The Concert

Oil on wood, $17\frac{3}{8} \times 21\frac{5}{8}''$
Formerly Rumiantsev Museum, Moscow

Pieter Codde, an Amsterdam artist who developed his talent at Haarlem in the School of Frans Hals, is above all a genre painter. His favorite subjects are drawn from the domestic life of the burghers. Like this one, he produced a number of scenes often treated by Dutch painters.

It was probably executed during the first third of the seventeenth century. In that period Codde favored sparsely furnished rooms, leaving free space around the figures, most often shown busy at their everyday tasks. Here an effect of unity is achieved by the homely setting.

Only the attitudes of the musicians bring to mind the School of Haarlem. Codde does not go in for brilliant colors; the over-all tonality—olive brown—is not a bit altered by the splashes of black, white, and red. However, the work does have spontaneity and naturalness in common with the Haarlem masters.

PLATE 47

ADRIAEN VAN OSTADE

1610–84

The Flute Player

Oil on wood, 11⅜ × 9″
Formerly Rumiantsev Museum, Moscow

This serious-looking flute player, concentrating solely on his instrument, occupies a special place among the grotesque and occasionally freakish figures of peasants painted by Adriaen van Ostade, the famous Haarlem genre artist. The hat conceals part of the homely face; coarse fingers touch the flute caressingly. The figure is painted in small brush strokes, with loving meticulousness, against a lightly sketched background. The whole is bathed in an atmosphere of serenity. This is one of the most deeply felt portrayals of a rural musician in seventeenth-century Dutch painting.

Such a conception of the subject is characteristic of the artist's late period, when he sometimes renounced grotesqueness and exaggeration and displayed a certain inclination for circumstantial narrative, with real sympathy for the figures represented. The cool gray-blue tones, and the detailed handwriting suggest that the work was not executed before the 1650s. By then the artist's favorite type of composition—a single figure shown half-size or down to the knees—took definitive form. This *Flute Player* is one of the finest and most original examples.

PLATE 48

REMBRANDT VAN RIJN

1606–69

Ahasuerus, Haman, and Esther

Oil on canvas, 28¾ × 37″ · Formerly Rumiantsev Museum, Moscow

In accordance with tradition, Rembrandt shows the heroes of the Biblical story seated around a table. Esther accuses Haman of having slandered her people and doomed them to die.

Rembrandt has chosen to paint the moment when Esther has made her accusation, and the king has not yet made up his mind. The characters are tense, motionless, each absorbed in his own thoughts. Esther has lowered her eyes; Haman, deeply shaken, is waiting for the king to decide his fate; the king is silent, pondering.

Esther is the central figure of the painting. Rembrandt deploys all the resources of his art and all his capacity to charm in portraying her.

The mysteriously dark background, the flamboyant colors in the foreground, every splotch of color, and every brush stroke express the mood of expectant decision. This 1660 work is an example of Rembrandt's mastery in his old age.

PLATE 49

REMBRANDT VAN RIJN

1606–69

Portrait of Adriaen van Rijn, the Artist's Brother

Oil on canvas, 29⅛ × 24¾″ · Formerly The Hermitage, Leningrad

Portraits of Adriaen van Rijn are to be seen in The Louvre, the museums of Berlin and The Hague, as well as in the Pushkin Museum. All four of them were painted by Rembrandt in the early 1650s. It is generally believed that the sitter was the artist's brother, a cobbler in Leiden who inherited the family mill. The strongest argument against this opinion is the scarcely legible date on the portrait in Moscow—1654—for Rembrandt's brother died in 1652. Nor can it be claimed that the portrait is posthumous, painted from memory, for those who have seen the picture itself rather than reproductions of it are impressed by its concreteness. The figure is shown seated, pensive, eyes turned slightly away from the golden evening sunlight, the reflections of which glide softly over his face. The figure is so "alive," it is hard to believe it was not painted from a model.

PLATE 50

REMBRANDT VAN RIJN

1606–69

Portrait of an Old Woman

Oil on canvas, 29⅛ × 24¾″ · Formerly The Hermitage, Leningrad

Some historians believe that this portrait is a companion piece to the portrait of the artist's brother. But the color reproduction shows how different the two works are, not only in respect to color, but also in treatment and atmosphere. It is hard to believe they were meant to be paired. However, even though the sitter was probably not Rembrandt's sister-in-law, she must have been a close friend, for she turns up in several of his works.

In this portrait, which displays all the characteristic features of his last period, Rembrandt attains the peak of his art. The colors are somber, the face is flooded with light, and psychological complexity and insight are evident. This woman is no mere model posing; she seems to be unaware of her surroundings, wholly caught up in private thoughts and memories. When we study her face, we can divine that her life was filled with care and sorrow, and we feel her courage and profound wisdom.

This is one of a number of Rembrandts that justify the claim that no painter has ever surpassed Rembrandt in portraying man's inner life. The work is signed and dated 1654.

PLATE 51

EMANUEL DE WITTE

1617–92

Waterfront Market

Oil on canvas, 24 × 29½″ · Formerly Kursk Museum

This work, de Witte's masterpiece, was discovered in 1930, among a number of time-darkened canvases by obscure painters in the reserves of the Kursk Museum. When the precise outlines and sonorous colors emerged from under the layers of varnish, it became clear that this was one of the few, but justly famous, genre scenes by an artist mostly known for his church interiors.

De Witte has not treated this traditional Dutch genre theme as the minor Dutch masters did. The precision of the outlines, the clear light, and the well-defined colors are characteristic of his more monumental style. The violent contrasts of dimension in the figures combine with the contrasts between light and dark to suggest space and define volumes.

This is one of de Witte's most intensely dramatic works. The alternation of patches of bright light color with heavy shadows creates a rather disquieting atmosphere. A saturated green stands out amidst blacks and dark grays; the white area seems to give off a certain radiance.

This is certainly one of the finest specimens of the works of de Witte, whose talent developed in contact with the School of Delft. It was probably executed in the late 1660s or the early 1670s in Amsterdam, where the artist worked after spending ten years at Delft.

PLATE 52

PIETER DE HOOCH

1629–c. 1685

Young Man Dressing

Oil on canvas, 25¾ × 20⅞″ · Formerly The Hermitage, Leningrad

The morning sun is just beginning to light up a poorly furnished bedroom. A young man is slowly pulling his boots on, while a servant girl makes the bed. The famous Dutch genre painter Pieter de Hooch thus re-creates an everyday scene and does not hesitate to show us the most prosaic details. This work is painted in short, rapid brush strokes, hastily superimposed, in yellow and pink tones much more brilliant than is customary with this artist. The room is bathed in air and light. Sincerely fond of cozy domestic scenes like this one, the painter communicates his pleasure in celebrating everyday life.

This is most likely an early work, executed shortly before he arrived in Delft and became acquainted with the works of local artists, such as Karel Fabritius, who we know influenced him.

The vicissitudes of this work in Russia are interesting. Prince Trubetskoy thought it was a portrait of Peter the Great made during the latter's visit to Holland, and he offered it as such to Czar Alexander I. The error was early recognized, but the painter was not identified until the end of the last century. It is today considered one of de Hooch's most original works.

PLATE 53

JACOB VAN RUISDAEL

1628–82

View of the Village of Egmont

Oil on wood, 17¾ × 14⅝″ · Formerly Collection Shuvalova, Leningrad

The abrupt bend in the road and the rolling hills lead the viewer's eye to the square church tower, surrounded by tiled roofs, in the background. Here and there light breaks through the heavy clouds to spill down spots of brightness on the road, on the chalky dunes at the back, and on the sea. Bathed in a stormy, restless atmosphere, this landscape expresses Ruisdael's conception of nature as perpetual movement, as a struggle between grandiose forces, a conflict between heterogeneous elements, each with its own individuality.

The village of Egmont with its typical church tower appears in a number of compositions by this artist. The high horizon line (it is as though we are looking down from a hilltop), the effect of perspective brought out by the bend in the road, the contrast between darker and lighter masses—all this is characteristic of Ruisdael's manner.

The landscape shown here has always been considered an authentic work by Ruisdael. Recently, however, its attribution has aroused certain doubts, despite the fact that when it was restored a short time ago the artist's monogram was revealed. Although the colors are those of the great landscape painter in his last period, the execution seems to be unusually dry, fragmentary, and lacking in vigor. Be that as it may, we find in this work the dramatic conception of the landscape, of which Ruisdael was the leading representative in Holland.

ENGLISH SCHOOL

PLATE 54

THOMAS LAWRENCE

1769–1830

Portrait of Sally Siddons

Oil on canvas, 15¾ × 13⅜″ · Formerly Tretyakov Gallery, Moscow

This portrait is very different from the official portraits to which Lawrence owed his celebrity. The freshness of execution and naturalness of the figure lend the painting a special charm. We see a young woman, almost a girl, whose serious eyes gaze expressively at the viewer. Their moist brilliance has the quality that Delacroix so greatly admired in Lawrence's portraits. The work seems to have been executed in 1795 or 1796, when the sitter was twenty years of age.

Sally Siddons, daughter of the famous tragic actress, Sarah Siddons, was engaged to marry the painter. Suddenly he became infatuated with her younger sister, Mary. Sally gave way to her sister without protest, but the artist's marriage with Mary did not take place, because she fell ill with consumption. Feeling that her days were numbered, and that her fickle fiancé might return to his first love, Mary made Sally swear that she would never be Lawrence's wife. Despite the artist's prayers, Sally kept her promise to her dying sister. In 1803 she too died of consumption, only four years after Mary.

PLATE 55

THOMAS LAWRENCE

1769–1830

Portrait of Countess Vorontsova

Pencil, sanguine, and chalk on canvas, 28⅜ × 24¾"
Formerly Collection Shchukin, Moscow

The artist's pencil re-creates the face of the attractive young woman whom Pushkin loved and celebrated in verse. The Countess Elizaveta Ksaveerevna Vorontsova was twenty-one when Thomas Lawrence drew her portrait in 1821. She had gone to London with her husband to visit his father, the aged Count Vorontsov, who served as Russian ambassador to England for twenty years. Lawrence had previously painted the ambassador, and now he executed a large portrait of his son, the brilliant young General Vorontsov, and at the same time sketched this likeness of the latter's wife. The canvas, sized with white paint and lightly touched with sanguine and chalk, seems to be barely grazed by the drawing; the delicate lines endow the young woman's features with an almost ethereal grace. Perfect execution is combined with the spontaneity of a rapid sketch.

This drawing is typical of the pencil portrait, a genre created and cultivated by Lawrence who was by nature a draftsman rather than a painter. He began his career as a portraitist with small pencil drawings, and later, when he painted portraits, always drew them first on the canvas in full detail. In his maturity Lawrence assembled one of the finest collections in his day of drawings by old masters.

This portrait, striking in its exquisite artistry and masterful execution, is a magnificent example of Lawrence's portrait drawings.

PLATE 56

JOHN CONSTABLE

1776–1837

View of Highgate

Oil on cardboard, 9½ × 11½″ · Formerly State Museum Reserves, Leningrad

Highgate, today a populous section of London, in Constable's day was, like its neighboring Hampstead, no more than a picturesque village with ponds and verdant hills. Constable often went there to paint and in 1826 bought a house in Hampstead, where he stayed until his death.

Scenes of Hampstead, which occupy an important place in his work, inspired some of his finest compositions. Most date from the early 1830s, his mature period. At that time Constable executed a number of small-sized paintings done directly from nature, in which a vigorous, personal style is combined with accurate observation, and freshness and spontaneity of impression with monumental perfection of composition. *View of Highgate* is one of these paintings.

This modest work strikes us by the depth and vigor of its realism. The artist marvelously suggests vast space, leading the eye over low hills to the distant village. The intense colors—the dark green vegetation, the rusty red patches of soil, the various shades of gray in the clouded sky—display all the richness and power of Constable's palette. Despite its size, this work is a fine example of Constable's art, one of the sources of nineteenth-century realist landscapes.

FRENCH SCHOOL

PLATE 57

NICOLAS POUSSIN

1594–1665

Joshua's Victory Over the Amorites

Oil on canvas, $30\frac{1}{4} \times 24\frac{3}{8}''$ · Formerly The Hermitage, Leningrad

Poussin spent almost all his life in Italy, but his long stay abroad did not alter the national character of his art. He is one of the most authentic and accomplished representatives of the French genius, a rationalist who expressed lofty philosophical ideas in harmonious paintings. He is justly considered the leader of French seventeenth-century classicism. Imitation of antiquity was, as is well known, an essential feature of classicism; but each artist assimilated classical art in his own way. Poussin's creative method can scarcely be called imitative, although he did draw sarcophagi and details from triumphal arches and the Trajan column.

The painting shown here is of special interest because it was composed in the period when Poussin was just discovering antiquity, shortly after his arrival in Rome in 1625. The influence of Roman bas-relief is especially reflected in the composition: successive planes rise one behind the other as they recede in depth, so that the last plane with the smallest and flattest figures comes close to the upper edge of the canvas. It will be noted that the Biblical warriors wear Roman armor and accouterments.

This work is a companion piece to the painting *Joshua's Victory Over the Amalekites* in The Hermitage. The composition is executed predominantly in austere browns, with only a few silvery reflections and combinations of blue and golden tones more characteristic of Poussin's later works. These paintings, acquired by Catherine II in the eighteenth century, aroused special interest at the Poussin exhibition in The Louvre in 1960.

PLATE 58

CLAUDE LORRAIN

1600–82

The Rape of Europa

Oil on canvas, 39⅜ × 53⅞″ · Formerly The Hermitage, Leningrad

This work is one of the finest of the many Claude Lorrains in the Soviet Union. Painted in 1655 for Pope Alexander VII, it has been copied many times. The best and most faithful copy, executed by Claude Lorrain himself, is in Buckingham Palace.

As usual with Claude Lorrain, the subject—the story of Europa carried off by Zeus, who has been transformed into a bull—is of secondary importance. The little figures in the foreground serve primarily to introduce the viewer into the radiantly poetic atmosphere of the ancient myth, whose spirit seems to pervade the noble landscape bathed in limpid light. Under the luminous sky the sapphire-colored sea spreads into the distance. The majestic trees partly conceal the horizon and the diaphanous mountain peaks in the background.

In his landscapes Claude Lorrain never tried to render the exact appearance of a specific site. He chose nature's most beautiful elements and brought them together in harmonious, well-balanced compositions. A great master of classical landscape, he was at the same time a great innovator. By his treatment of air and light he blazed new trails in landscape painting.

PLATE 59

ANTOINE WATTEAU

1684–1721

Satire on Physicians

Oil on wood, 10¼ × 14⅝″ · Formerly The Hermitage, Leningrad

Watteau's art was closely associated with the theater, whose fairylike, capricious world fascinated the artist throughout his lifetime. His paintings teem with figures and scenes taken from French and Italian comedies. He depicts with sympathy the melancholy adventures of Gilles and Mezzetino, and is inspired by farcical scenes as in this charming little painting known as *Satire on Physicians*. The subject may be a scene from Molière's *Le Malade imaginaire*: the line "What have I done, you accursed murderers?" ("*Qu' ai-je fait, assassins maudits?*") from that play was formerly the title of this work.

A man in a dressing gown and nightcap is shown fleeing from a group of physicians and apothecaries threatening him with enema tubes. The comical procession seems to be on a stage against the backdrop of a cemetery with tombs and sarcophagi, which allude to the sad fate awaiting the patient.

This is one of Watteau's earliest works, but we can already discern the main features of his style—the fragile grace of the figures, the drawing at once light and accurate, the faded colors, and the exquisite play of subtle tonal harmonies, none of which were to be found in the preceding generation of painters.

Delicate irony tinged with a strange sadness pervades this comical little scene, endowing it with the peculiar charm that distinguishes Watteau's art.

PLATE 60

FRANÇOIS LEMOYNE

1688–1737

The Rape of Europa

Oil on canvas, 28⅜ × 23⅝"
Formerly Collection Prince Yusupov, Leningrad

An exquisite, blond Europa, surrounded by companions who are adorning her with flowers, is seated on the back of a bull. Above the group, an amoretto is clinging to the branch of a tree. At the right, a bright blue sky is suspended over the sea where the bull is about to carry off the imprudent beauty. The scene is treated with casual ease. The nacreous flesh of the girls and their light clothing stirred by the breeze are gracefully rendered. Their waving arms and wreaths of flowers form capricious arabesques.

In this painting, signed and dated 1725, we find all the features of the Rococo—a refined decorative sense; bright, elegant coloring; light, flexible brush strokes; freedom in the portrayal of movement. The composition brings to mind the central group in Veronese's *Rape of Europa* in the Palace of the Doges, which Lemoyne probably saw on his visit to Venice in 1724.

Lemoyne executed many easel paintings, mostly on amorous subjects drawn from mythology. He is also known for his large decorative compositions. The most famous of these is the Hercules ceiling at Versailles, which he completed in 1736.

PLATE 61

FRANÇOIS BOUCHER

1703–70

Hercules and Omphale

Oil on canvas, $35\frac{3}{8} \times 29\frac{1}{8}''$
Formerly The Hermitage, Leningrad

Director of the Academy and "First Painter to the King,"
Boucher brilliantly expressed the ideals and artistic tastes of
eighteenth-century society. This "painter of the graces" produced a large number of colorful mural panels, ladies' fans,
cartoons for tapestries, mythological, religious, and pastoral
scenes, portraits in oils, and landscapes.

Hercules and Omphale is a good example of the period's pre-
occupation with the erotic, concealed, as it were, under a
mythological mask. In this painting Boucher makes use of alle-
gory, a current academic device in his day. A distaff (symbol
of feminine virtue) and a lion's skin (symbol of masculine
valor) are being held by the two amoretti. Sensual passion,
however, is expressed so vividly that the allegorical commen-
tary is superfluous. Boucher delights us with his refined color
harmonies. The faded red curtain against the gray wall, the
gilded furniture, the bluish-white of the sheets, and the soft
pink of Omphale's body form a decorative composition typical of the Rococo style.

PLATE 62

JEAN-BAPTISTE-SIMÉON CHARDIN

1693–1779

The Attributes of the Arts

Oil on canvas, 20½ × 44⅛″ · Formerly The Hermitage, Leningrad

In the second half of the eighteenth century the increasing strength of the French middle class was reflected in the gradual rise to dignity and importance of realistic painting. This art stressed the humble, everyday truths, in marked contrast to the brilliant but lifeless art of the court.

In his genre scenes and still lifes Chardin stresses the values of the material and historical world. The painting shown here is distinguished by its simplicity, balanced composition, and clearly defined forms. This bespeaks a very different approach to reality from that of the Rococo painters with their complicated, fragile forms and their fictional subjects. Similarly, Chardin's palette is very different from the elegant, bright coloring of the Rococo style. In this work we find a calm but austere range of subdued silvery tones and a subtle combination of values.

This work represents a special type of still life, the objects having been assembled to symbolize the arts and sciences. There are similar examples of this type: *The Attributes of the Arts* in the Hermitage, *The Attributes of Music* in The Louvre, *The Attributes of the Sciences* in the Jacquemart-André Museum, and in other places.

PLATE 63

JEAN-HONORÉ FRAGONARD

1732–1806

Savoyard with Kerchief

Oil on copper, $12\frac{1}{4} \times 9\frac{1}{2}''$ · Formerly Collection Prince Yusupov, Leningrad

There is a tradition according to which this little Savoyard with her round pink face and sparkling, roguish eyes is a portrait of the artist's daughter, Rosalie. Fragonard never cared for the solemn type of official portraits done on commission in a ready-made pattern. But he often portrayed friends and members of his family, representing them as romantic figures full of life and movement, and he repeatedly introduced their features into his little genre scenes.

There are several variants of the work shown here, the best of them in the Wildenstein Collection. The Albertina in Vienna owns a watercolor study for this painting.

PLATE 64

JACQUES-LOUIS DAVID

1748–1825

Portrait of a Young Man

Oil on canvas, 21¼ × 18⅛″ · Formerly Tretyakov Gallery, Moscow

David was one of the best French portraitists. His portraits brilliantly display the realistic spirit of his art, his supreme ability to produce images of universal appeal that combine psychological insight with clear-cut social characterization.

This portrait was acquired in Paris late in the nineteenth century; at that time it was erroneously entitled *Portrait of the Young Ingres*. Whatever the identity of the sitter, David succeeded in creating a portrait that delineates a whole generation. What we see here is a young man of the early nineteenth century, such as we encounter in the works of Stendhal, Balzac, and Musset —ardent, energetic, stubborn, yet already corroded by disillusionment and doubt; eager to achieve "great deeds," yet feeling cheated of the great hopes that had been aroused by the revolutionary ideals. Because the artist was successful in rendering the sitter's inner conflicts and complexity, the work is an authentic masterpiece of the psychological portrait.

PLATE 65

ANTOINE-JEAN GROS

1771–1835

Portrait of Prince Yusupov in Tatar Costume

Oil on canvas, 126⅜ × 104¾″
Formerly Collection Prince Yusupov, Leningrad

Antoine-Jean Gros, the famous painter of battle scenes, is represented in Soviet museums only by portraits, among them the work shown here. Despite a certain official coldness, it displays romantic traits. Commissioned by Prince Nikolai Borisovich Yusupov, a great lover of art, this painting represents the prince's son, Boris Nikolaevich, then thirteen years old. The boy is wearing a Tatar costume in honor of the founder of the Yusupov family, Ysuv Murza, who was descended from the khans of the Golden Horde. The white Maltese cross pinned to the fur-bordered jacket is a reminder that in 1799 the prince was appointed Commander of the Order of St. John of Jerusalem.

This portrait of 1809 was listed in the catalogue of the Gros exhibition held in Paris in 1935.

PLATE 66

EUGÈNE DELACROIX

1798–1863

After the Shipwreck

Oil on canvas, 14⅛ × 22½″ · Formerly Tretyakov Gallery, Moscow

This is the only Delacroix in the Pushkin Museum. Small as it is, however, the canvas perfectly expresses the tragic, tormented genius of the great Romantic painter. A small boat is drifting rudderless; two of its occupants lie prostrate, while two others are about to throw overboard the body of a companion. The dark green waves almost merge with the dark blue clouds hanging low over the sea; here and there patches of red and white in the clothing erupt to set off violent contrasts.

Baudelaire admired Delacroix's ability to endow his colors with an expressiveness specially adapted to the subject and atmosphere of the painting. "Color is nothing unless it intensifies the painting's effect on the imagination," Delacroix wrote. This work could almost have been painted to illustrate the statement.

Throughout his life Delacroix was fascinated by the theme of man's dramatic conflict with the elements. The conception and execution of this work bring to mind the celebrated *Last Scene of Don Juan* of 1841 and it certainly dates from the same period.

PLATE 67

CHARLES-FRANÇOIS DAUBIGNY

1817–78

Village on the Banks of the Oise

Oil on wood, 38⅛ × 26″ · Formerly Tretyakov Gallery, Moscow

Born into a family of artists, Daubigny belonged to an intellectual milieu that championed democracy. His social sympathies were expressed with particular clarity after 1840, when this political movement began to gain strength. He founded a small group in Paris whose members undertook to help one another secure favorable working conditions. Each in turn painted a work that could be accepted by the Salon, while the others executed profitable commissions, putting the proceeds into a common fund.

Daubigny's trips into the French countryside, particularly along the Oise, played an important role in his life. It is hard to say whether the artist was not more fond of nature than of painting. Only someone who had long and lovingly contemplated the slow rhythm of life along the banks of a river could have painted a work like this *Village on the Banks of the Oise*, dated 1860.

Daubigny's landscapes are extremely varied. The features of the place represented, as well as the meteorological conditions of the moment, determine the dominant colors and even the character of his brush stroke. In the course of time Daubigny's works became more and more sketchlike. From 1860 on he was preoccupied with problems of light and color, and by his approach to them he reveals himself a precursor of Impressionism.

PLATE 68

VIRGILE-NARCISSE DIAZ DE LA PEÑA

1807–76

The Approaching Storm

Oil on wood, 8¼ × 11¾″ · Formerly Rumiantsev Museum, Moscow

Diaz de la Peña, though of Spanish descent, was born in Bordeaux. He lost his parents at an early age and was obliged to support himself. He worked in the national ceramics factory at Sèvres as a painter of china.

As a young man he became passionately interested in the art of Prud'hon and Correggio. His earliest works are Venuses, graceful nymphs, and plump Cupids frolicking in sun-drenched clearings in the woods. However, he soon gave up this kind of composition for more truthful renderings of his native landscape. He moved to Barbizon, where he met Millet and Theodore Rousseau.

In his paintings of the 1860s and early 1870s he shows himself a master of the realistic landscape, excelling especially in views of sparse, sunlit woods. He never painted nature in spring or in winter, preferring the brilliant light of summer and the sumptuous colors of autumn. In this work of 1871 the black, wind-swept clouds create a tense, Romantic atmosphere. The tiny figure of a woman hurrying to shelter before the impending storm breaks accentuates this feeling, while the golden-yellow foliage enhances the dark blue of the sky. Color plays an important part in Diaz de la Peña's works; the artist made an effort to banish somber hues from his palette.

PLATE 69

JEAN-BAPTISTE-CAMILLE COROT

1796–1875

The Belfry at Argenteuil

Oil on canvas, 10⅝ × 6¾″ · Formerly Rumiantsev Museum, Moscow

The work shown here dates from the late 1850s, when Corot's painting was disclosing features that herald Impressionism. To an ever greater extent he employed a technique of lightly applied brush strokes, masterfully interwoven, blurring the outlines of objects and figures. In his landscapes, however, the disposition of the various planes remains strictly classical, the alternation of light and dark producing an illusion of depth.

Corot was deeply sensitive to the poetry of nature, and at the same time aimed at truthful rendering. *The Belfry at Argenteuil* is a good example of his style. Autumnal calm bathes this peaceful village street. A few brush strokes serve to render the figures of the women and children, and yet the figures are none the less expressive. They seem to be savoring the morning freshness under a sky sparkling with silvery clouds.

Corot painted "naïvely and without trickery." He did not seek out public recognition, and it was a long time in coming to him. Entirely devoted to his art, he led a modest life, the only outward events of which were a few long stays in Italy and frequent trips around the French countryside.

PLATE 70

JEAN-FRANÇOIS MILLET

1814–75

Women Gathering Wood

Oil on canvas, 14⅝ × 17¾″ · Formerly Tretyakov Gallery, Moscow

Jean-François Millet, a brilliant representative of democratic, realist art, described himself in the following terms: "I am a peasant, just a peasant."

This statement defines the essential theme of his art as well as his origin—he was the son of a Norman peasant. Familiar with work in the fields from personal experience, Millet treats peasant life in a simple, honest manner, without sentimentalism or "pastoral" affectation. His paintings express love for the humble beauty of his native countryside, a love that is rooted in childhood memories.

In 1849 he settled in Barbizon, where he was closely associated with the so-called "Barbizon School" of landscape painters. But his art is very different from theirs. Millet's landscapes are rooted in the labor of the countryside: work in fields, gardens, and woods. When he portrays the forest—as he does in the work shown here—he takes the viewer right to the heart of it. Here only the lower parts of the trees appear. The sloping hill in the foreground is typical; its diagonal determines the positions and movement of the two women shown dragging a long branch of fallen timber.

Millet models forms and volumes and defines depth with irregular, bold brush strokes. The warm, vibrant browns that predominate in this work are characteristic of his mature period, the late 1850s, when his talent had been universally recognized.

GUSTAVE COURBET

1819–77

Chalet in the Mountains

Oil on canvas, 13 × 19¼″ · Formerly Museum of Modern Western Art, Moscow

Son of a wine grower in Ornans, Courbet called himself "a student of nature." He was the leading champion of realism. Because of his popularity he was elected to the Chamber under the Commune. This made serious trouble for him later, when the government of the Third Republic held him responsible for the destruction of the Vendôme column. He was put on trial and fined a large sum. He escaped to Switzerland, where he died at La Tour du Peilz. The signed work shown here dates from his last years. At this time he was seeking spiritual solace in nature after the upsets and disappointments of political life, and landscape became his favorite genre.

Chalet in the Mountains is a masterpiece of this genre. Here Courbet achieves unity of artistic expression—something he often failed to achieve. The work reveals deep insight into the austere beauty of this mountainous region. Courbet succeeds in conveying an impression of immense space on a small canvas. The snow-capped peaks form a gigantic amphitheater. The viewer feels the wavy rise of the foothills in the middle distance. The modest chalet seems to be hugging the slope of the hill behind it for protection. There are no human figures. The presence of man is indicated only by the multicolored laundry fluttering in the wind. These bright spots introduce sonorous tones into the austere scale of grays, browns, and greens that serve to render nature's more grandiose aspects.

PLATE 72

EUGÈNE BOUDIN

1824–98

Beach at Trouville

Oil on wood, 7½ × 18⅛″ · Formerly Collection P. D. Ettinger, Moscow

The narrow horizontal format of the painting determines the very simple composition. The horizon line passes midway. The pearly-gray, transparently cloudy zone of the sky touches the gray-blue zone of the sea. Below it extends the flat sandy beach. Against the background of the sea there is a frieze-like group of men and women. The faces are barely indicated; figures, hats, clothing are rendered casually, but everything has been observed so accurately that the viewer at once recognizes the fashions of the early 1870s, even without consulting the date at the lower left (1871). This date is suggested above all by the artist's technique. The colors are subordinated to the dominant tone—the silvery-gray mist of the damp atmosphere. The colors of the clothing echo the bluish sea and the sandy beach. One black, one white, and two red accents animate the group.

Everything in this painting shows that Boudin was an organic link in the development of Impressionism, marking the transition to it from the Barbizon landscape painters, especially Troyon. He greatly admired Corot. He helped Claude Monet find himself, disclosing to him the beauty of seascapes and the exquisite colors concealed in nature.

PLATE 73

CAMILLE PISSARRO

1830–1903

Avenue de l'Opéra

Oil on canvas, 25⅝ × 32¼″
Formerly Museum of Modern Western Art, Moscow

Camille Pissarro, the oldest of the Impressionists, was born on the island of St. Thomas in the West Indies. He studied in Paris, then went home to work as a clerk in his father's store. At the age of twenty-five he returned to France. After meeting Claude Monet at the Swiss Academy, he began to employ the new Impressionist technique. His works dating from this period are distinguished by simplicity of subject, refinement of color, and poetic mood. In the 1880s the artist came under the influence of Seurat and Signac. The Divisionist experiments left a durable imprint on his art: the chromatic scale became even more refined.

The painting shown here, dated 1898, comes from the artist's last period, when he primarily painted views of Paris. Unable to work out-of-doors because of an eye ailment, he worked in a studio overlooking the Avenue de l'Opéra. He painted two versions of it: one on a clear sunny day (Museum of Fine Arts in Belgrade), and this one under gray skies. The very delicately shaded silvery-grays, pinks, and blues render the glistening pavement in which are reflected the lowering skies. The moist air that envelops everything in shimmering mist is rendered with delicate, quivering brush strokes. The stream of fiacres and the hurrying figures of pedestrians express the animation of a big city's bustling life.

PLATE 74

HENRI DE TOULOUSE-LAUTREC

1864–1901

Yvette Guilbert

Color lithograph on cardboard, $22\frac{1}{2} \times 16\frac{1}{2}''$
Formerly Museum of Modern Western Art, Moscow

Unlike Cézanne, Van Gogh, and Gauguin, Toulouse-Lautrec was never drawn to landscapes. He was fond of the life of cafés, bars, and theaters, the world of actors, ballerinas, and circus performers. His studies at Bonnat's school and the Cormon studio were short-lived; his true masters were Degas, Forain, and the nineteenth-century Japanese artists.

He was fond of the expressive line, the nervous silhouette, the refined spot of color. He looked at the world with bitter irony and pitiless cynicism. His aesthetic ideal was entirely personal, and his heroes are highly unusual—they are ugly, sometimes repulsively vulgar, and a little comical.

Lautrec drew Yvette Guilbert in November, 1894. At the time, he was a contributor to *Le Rire*, a weekly founded by Arsène Alexandre. Yvette Guilbert, a singer, was then at the height of her celebrity. All Paris was familiar with her dead-white clownlike make-up, her red hair, her tight-fitting green dress, her long black gloves. Lautrec never missed one of her performances if he could help it. He drew her singing on the stage, sticking her head out through the curtain, and dashing hurriedly out of a restaurant, umbrella in hand. The present drawing is a variant of one published in *Le Rire*, No. 7, for December 24, 1894. Another version is to be found in the portfolio titled *Yvette Guilbert;* it dates from the same year.

PLATE 75

EDGAR DEGAS

1834–1917

Dancers in Blue

Pastel, 25½ × 26″ · Formerly Museum of Modern Western Art, Moscow

Degas took part in the first Impressionist exhibition and was a champion of pure color. He sought to recapture the fugitive moment of visual perception by making his compositions seem (the one shown here is an example) to have been arbitrarily cut off by the frame. On the whole, he went his own way, however. Unlike the Impressionists, he was less interested in the brilliant light of out-of-doors than in the more diffuse daylight as seen indoors or the artificial light of the theater stage, which alters contours and forms. He was above all intent on capturing the movements of the human body, especially those based on long professional training.

Degas' favorite subjects were jockeys, musicians, laundresses, and ballet dancers. He depicts the dance as a hard taskmaster, and most often his dancers are shown offstage, in the wings, in their dressing rooms, or practicing at the bar. Their expressions are tired or indifferent, though they are attractive in their own way. Degas mostly worked in pastel, employing bold color combinations that harmonized with the sharpness of his drawing—the latter was to him the main thing. He was also interested in sculpture, and tried to capture the fugitive beauty of human movement in plastic terms. This picture was executed between 1900 and 1905.

PLATE 76

AUGUSTE RENOIR

1841–1919

La Grenouillère

Oil on canvas, 23¼ × 31½"
Formerly Museum of Modern Western Art, Moscow

Renoir's landscapes profoundly influenced painters of outdoor scenes. The work shown here, dating from the late 1860s, discloses how sure the Impressionists were of the validity of their approach long before the first group exhibition in 1874. It is simply amazing to see how easily Renoir, who had started his career painting amorous scenes on ceramics, captures the real face of nature, the joyous animation of a holiday crowd.

In the 1860s La Grenouillère was a popular river resort near Paris, a frequent goal of weekend excursions. Claude Monet also painted it, and a little later de Maupassant used it as a setting for short stories. Renoir does not portray it from any fixed point of view, such as might be identified by a visitor to the place. What interested him was the color symphony composed by the water, the sky, the green foliage, the clothes of the excursionists, and the play of sunshine and shadow. A white sail sparkles in the sun and spots of sunshine dapple the women's umbrellas and belts with bright blues and reds. Silhouettes of half-nude bathers are seen in the water. When we look closely at the painting, the contours of the objects dissolve, the forms break up, and all that remains are brush strokes of great freedom and originality applied with a sureness and accuracy that only a great master could achieve.

PLATE 77

AUGUSTE RENOIR

1841–1919

Portrait of Jeanne Samary

Oil on canvas, 22 × 18½″
Formerly Museum of Modern Western Art, Moscow

This work figured in the Impressionist Exhibition of 1877. Portraits occupy a more important place in Renoir's painting than in that of other Impressionists. He was especially fond of depicting feminine figures of a sensual, fresh, tender beauty. He made several portraits of Jeanne Samary, an actress who made a successful debut at the Théâtre Français in 1875, as Dorine in Molière's *Tartuffe*. In her short lifetime she invariably aroused enthusiasm by her subtle, lively acting, musical laugh, and perfect diction.

The present portrait, a preliminary study for the full-sized portrait in The Hermitage, is distinguished by its freshness and spontaneity. Renoir has not tried to render the psychology of the twenty-year-old actress. Her smile is no more than an expression of conventional politeness, though a spark of playfulness can be discerned in her eyes. Her joy in life, her awareness of her youth, beauty, talent, and success are conveyed in a sonorous harmony of bright colors. The pinks do not just serve as background, they also envelop the figure like a cloud, out of which she emerges gracefully in a blue dress, with sparkling auburn hair and fresh cheeks. Her lipstick is the same color as the rose at her shoulder.

PLATE 78

CLAUDE MONET

1840–1926

Le Déjeuner sur l'herbe

Oil on canvas, 51⅛ × 136⅝″
Formerly Museum of Modern Western Art, Moscow

This work is an important one, both in Monet's own development and in the history of Impressionism. It shows us how painting liberated itself from the dark colors of the academic school and a new vision asserted itself. The title of Monet's painting, *Impression: Rising Sun*, which was shown at the first Impressionist exhibition in 1874 is at the origin of the name eventually given the whole movement. It is interesting to note that in Monet's letters and memoirs, when he speaks of his teachers and friends, he often points out how they influenced his development and helped him perfect his approach to nature.

As a young man in Le Havre and the surrounding countryside, he discovered how the light changes in the humid air of the Norman coast. There he met his first teacher, Boudin, whose influence on him Monet himself acknowledged: "At last my eyes were opened. I really understood nature, and at the same time I learned to love it." He also mentions with gratitude his two years of military service in Algeria: "You cannot imagine how I increased my knowledge and how my vision benefited from it."

In April, 1865, perhaps inspired by the monumental dimensions of Courbet's *Stone Breakers*, Monet conceived a grandiose landscape—21′ × 21′ 1⅞″—to be entitled *Le Déjeuner sur l'herbe*, the main subject of which was to be sunlight in the woods. This canvas was later cut up into several parts: the left portion is in the Museum of Impressionism in Paris, and the central part is in a private collection.

The 1866 painting in the Pushkin Museum is the main preliminary study for this work; it was done from nature in the Fontainebleau forest. Among the figures two can be identified: they are the painters Lambrin (seated left) and Brazille (reclining under a tree to the right). The color pattern on the big tree trunk—velvety grays and greenish-browns—seems to determine the chromatic scale for the rest of the landscape and the clothing of the figures. The patches of blue sky glimpsed through the foliage are echoed in the women's dresses, especially in the blue scarf of the woman shown standing at the center. In the right foreground there are the bright spots of the red Scottish plaid and the green shawl. Everything is subordinated to the harmony of the sunlight. The artist did not shrink from rendering the fresh faces of the young women with a combination of greens, blue-grays, and brownish-grays. This new technique of "colored shadows" is also employed to render the sunlight as it filters through the green foliage. Iridescent spots animate the whites in the clothing and the tablecloth. The broad patches laid on with a palette knife run in different directions. We can scarcely recognize this as a preliminary drawing rather than a finished work. The brush stroke determines the colors and at the same time defines the contours and the forms.

PLATE 79

CLAUDE MONET

1840–1926

View of Vétheuil

Oil on canvas, 35⅜ × 36¼"
Formerly Museum of Modern Western Art, Moscow

This light-colored landscape, typical of late Impressionism, relates to Monet's London period (1901–03). At that time, he was fond of painting the light morning mist rising from the water and blurring the contours and volumes of objects. Here he shows us the houses of Vétheuil with their red tile roofs, clustered like a bouquet against the background greenery. This combination of colors is reflected in the water where it takes on new brilliance and vibrancy. The green willow at the bottom of the picture recalls Japanese color prints. The paint is applied thinly, and the canvas shows through in places. Characteristic of this period in Monet's development are the little horizontal brush strokes disposed in almost regular parallel rows, like a fabric or embroidery pattern.

PLATE 80

PAUL CÉZANNE

1839–1906

Le Jas de Bouffan

Oil on canvas, 28⅜ × 35⅞″ · Formerly Museum of Modern Western Art, Moscow

The rich collection of Cézannes in the Museum fully illustrates this painter's originality.

Le Jas de Bouffan was painted about 1885. It shows the little park adjoining the Cézannes' country house near Aix, where the artist lived and worked for over forty years (from 1853 to 1899). Like most of his other works, this landscape is not intended to be an accurate reproduction of a given site; nor does the artist seek to capture the reflections and nuances of light. His aim is to express the inherent qualities of nature. The color scheme is based on yellow, green, and blue—the colors respectively of the clayey, sun-parched soil of Provence, of grass and trees, and of the sky and distant horizons. Like the colors, the forms are divested of all ephemeral elements: the tree trunks are almost cylindrical; the mass of foliage is not differentiated; and the intersecting planes obey a rigorous geometry.

The slightly inclined surface of the soil, rendered with parallel brush strokes of equal dimensions in the foreground and the background, seems flat, without extension into depth. And yet the landscape clearly suggests three-dimensional space. This effect is achieved by the foreshortened wall at the left, the vanishing trees in the background, and, above all, by the alternating planes of warm orange and cool green. This is why the objects situated in the back of the picture seem at once distant and close. Similarly, the surface seems at once to be flat and deep. This gives Cézanne's space special intensity and dramatic power. Lionello Venturi called it "a miracle of art."

PLATE 81

PAUL CÉZANNE

1839–1906

The Banks of the Marne

Oil on canvas, 28 × 35⅜″ · Formerly Museum of Modern Western Art, Moscow

Whereas *Le Jas de Bouffan* illustrates Cézanne's creative method, *The Banks of the Marne* shows us the results of this method. It is a work of supreme excellence. The landscape, painted in 1888, that is, three or four years after the preceding one, is one of the master-pieces of Cézanne's mature period. The peaceful waters of the Marne guard like a treas-ure the reflected image of the real world, enhancing the massiveness and immobility of its forms. The dynamic lines of the banks are balanced and tempered by the tranquil and somewhat blurred reflections on the surface of the water. Nothing disturbs the solemn calm of the air and the river: nature seems frozen in an eternal immobility that is pregnant with profound meaning. The pigment, of a transparency that recalls water-color, is applied in easy, parallel brush strokes that do not hug closely the forms of the objects (as is the case with Van Gogh, for instance), but unify the various parts of the scene into a single homogeneous whole, conveying a sense of nature's infinity and objec-tive existence. Reflected in the water, nature itself seems to be a reflection of its own eter-nity and immutable laws.

PLATE 82

PAUL CÉZANNE

1839–1906

Mont Sainte-Victoire

Oil on canvas, 23⅝ × 28¾″
Formerly Museum of Modern Western Art, Moscow

This view of Mont Sainte-Victoire, near Aix, of which Cézanne painted several versions, dates from 1905, that is, from his last period. At that time he treated his motifs more freely than in his earlier paintings. The nervous, rapid strokes of thick paint construct the pictorial space. The distant parts of the landscape, painted a warm orange, seem closer, whereas the cool tones of the foreground produce an effect of distance. Thus the spatial planes are, so to speak, dislocated, with the result that the space seems concentrated, full of tension. Space has lost some of its three-dimensional, illusionary quality, but it has acquired a peculiar materiality. It seems to be moving toward the viewer from the depth of the picture, and becomes as tangible, voluminous, and heavy as the stony mass of the mountain. The sky, the mountain, and the plain seem to be compelled into impetuous movement by the dynamic brush strokes.

However, this movement that spreads in various directions and affects the various planes returns to its starting point, describes a complete cycle, closes in on itself, and stops, suggesting the dynamic peace of nature.

Cézanne's last landscapes are not representations of nature in the usual sense of the term. They do not observe the rules of perspective; the elements of proximity and distance, surface and volume, the static and the dynamic, are not clearly differentiated from each other. But they powerfully express the tension of nature, which includes all these heterogeneous elements and which absorbs into itself their concrete forms.

PLATE 83

VINCENT VAN GOGH

1853–90

The Red Vineyard (Arles)

Oil on canvas, 29½ × 36¼"
Formerly Museum of Modern Western Art, Moscow

It would be hard to find in all art history a painter whose fate was more tragic than Van Gogh's. Son of a Dutch pastor, he worked in Belgium and in France, and painted his earliest works in 1881. Ready to give his last crust of bread to any poor wretch he happened to meet, he spent his life in extreme poverty, just managing to survive, thanks to the help of his brother, Theo. All his works were created in less than ten years, during which time he did not succeed in selling a single painting. Unrecognized, ridiculed both by friends and enemies, he took his own life at the age of thirty-seven.

The work shown here is one of the finest of his last period. From his correspondence with his brother Theo and his friend Bernard, we learn that he painted it in 1888, during his stay at Arles. It was one of the works destined to decorate his little house there.

In Van Gogh's landscapes, nature seems like a living being, subject to joy, sorrow, and all the other human emotions. In *The Red Vineyard* one moment—nightfall—is transformed into a dramatic image of the struggle between night and day. Nature is caught up irresistibly in swirling movement by the tense, tormented lines of the horizon and the river. By keeping the point where these lines converge outside the canvas, Van Gogh enlarges the pictorial space, endowing it with a dynamic, cosmic quality, transforming it into an arena of struggle. The cool tones of the evening shadows—blue, green, and lavender—are gradually crowding out the warm daylight colors, as we move from left to right, and from the foreground to the background. The burning red and orange tones, applied in thick brush strokes that twist like flames, seem gradually to grow weaker, introducing a note of exhaustion into the tensely dramatic atmosphere of the painting as a whole.

PLATE 84

PAUL GAUGUIN

1848–1903

Landscape with Peacocks

Oil on canvas, 45¼ × 33⅞"
Formerly Museum of Modern Western Art, Moscow

Gauguin was born in Paris; his mother's ancestors were Spanish. Employed as a clerk to a Paris stockbroker, he began in the 1870s to paint in his leisure time. He associated with the Impressionists, bought their paintings, and later took part in their exhibitions. In 1883 he quit his job, separated from his family, and devoted himself entirely to painting. He often worked in Brittany, where he was surrounded by a group of painters known as the School of Pont-Aven (Sérusier, Bernard, Mauffrat). These artists were moving away from Impressionism, aiming at greater simplification and organization of the pictorial elements. For some time Gauguin stayed with Van Gogh at Arles. Later he made several trips to Polynesia.

From 1891 to 1893 he lived in Tahiti. Then, after spending some time in Europe, he returned to the South Seas where he lived like a native, first in Tahiti (1895–1901) and then on the island of Dominique, where he died in 1903.

In his works Gauguin aimed at monumentality and decorative color. Taking his subjects from local legends, he painted the life of the natives, idealizing it and endowing it with a solemn serenity. He stresses contours and silhouettes; figures and objects are traced in arabesques without highlights or shadows. The flat, segmented picture surface is divided into brightly colored areas. The composition is static, with harmonious combinations of tones. The silhouettes seem to be animated by a rhythmic movement.

The 1882 landscape shown here, entitled MATAMOE—a Tahitian word meaning "strangers"—is inspired by a legend: the proud strangers, that is to say, the peacocks, came to Tahiti after life had appeared on the island. The foreground, the distant mountains, and the hut are all covered with drawings in various colors. The fantastic entanglement of the trees with the red and orange spots of the foliage, the wisps of white smoke rising from the fire, the gracefully robust Tane chopping wood, the peacocks in the foreground—all these elements of the composition form a mosaic of color spots outlined in arabesques.

PLATE 85

PAUL GAUGUIN

1848–1903

The King's Wife

Oil on canvas, 38⅛ × 51⅛″ · Formerly Museum of Modern Western Art, Moscow

During his second trip to Tahiti, in 1896, Gauguin wrote to his friend Daniel de Monfreid, in a letter dated April 7: "I have just finished a canvas of 51⅛ × 39⅜″ which I think is better than anything so far: a queen reclining on a green rug, a servant picking fruit, two old men near the big tree discussing the tree of knowledge; seacoast in the background; this faint sketch executed with shaking hand will give you only a vague idea. I think that never before have I achieved such deep, sonorous colors. The trees are in flower, the dog is watchful, the two doves are cooing." This letter was illustrated with a pen sketch and a watercolor.

Gauguin was certainly right when he said that the colors of this painting are exceptionally rich and sonorous. The darker and lighter areas of the green grass harmonize marvelously with the brown body of the reclining woman. The warm areas formed by the red fan, the yellow bushes, and the pale blue water next to the pink sand shimmer like precious stones.

In the Shchukin Collection this painting was titled *Woman with Mangoes*, and it is still referred to under this title in books on Gauguin. However, the inscription in the Tahitian language, TE ARII VAHINE, means "the king's wife."

PLATE 86

PAUL GAUGUIN

1848–1903

The Parrots

Oil on canvas, 24⅜ × 28¾″ · Formerly Museum of Modern Western Art, Moscow

In this still life executed in 1902, that is, the year before his death, Gauguin renounces his broad, decorative style and goes back in part to Impressionist techniques. He combines his exotic subject (parrots sacrificed to Buddha) with a modern treatment of the still life.

The table is seen from above; the folds of the tablecloth are shown in volume, and each object is treated in a different manner. Shadows, absent in previous compositions, reappear here. The large areas representing the objects contrast with the light shadows they project on the tablecloth. The color white consists of a subtle play of blue and pink reflections. Spots of green, pink, blue, and orange applied in vibrant brush strokes render the plumage of the birds. Above the sumptuous lavender drawing surrounding the signature there is a luxuriant tropical flower enhanced with a rose. This still life is one of Gauguin's masterpieces.

PLATE 87

HENRI ROUSSEAU

1844–1910

The Muse Inspiring the Poet

Oil on canvas, 51⅝ × 38⅛″
Formerly Museum of Modern Western Art, Moscow

The Muse in this picture is the painter, Marie Laurencin; the poet is Guillaume Apollinaire, theoretician of Cubism and Rousseau's friend. The two figures are shown in frozen frontal attitudes surrounded by tropical vegetation; each leaf, meticulously drawn, seems to have the consistency of metal. The exaggerated facial features and inexact proportions introduce a caricatural element, although Rousseau painted his friends with eager sincerity and believed that his portraits were excellent likenesses. The flowers in the foreground are intended as a homage to the poet.

Rousseau painted the life of the Paris suburbs, adding genre scenes and fantastic tropical landscapes of his own invention. For a long time it was believed that he had visited Mexico as a soldier in his youth, but we know today that his inspiration for the luxuriant tropical vegetation came from visits to the botanical gardens.

Departing from the freedom of Impressionism, Rousseau strove for unity of composition and local color. He ignores the problems of aerial perspective, modeling, chiaroscuro, and movement. For all his technical clumsiness, his ignorance of the academic rules, and his dull, heavy colors, the monumental quality of his paintings comes through, and we can only admire the spontaneity, precision, sureness, and boldness of his pictorial idiom. In the work shown here the dark lavender of the dress harmonizes with the bright green plants and the naïve blue of the sky. This tonal combination brings to mind the shop signs, painted trays, and color prints of folk art.

This naïveté, plus certain elements of simplification and deformation, testify to an undeniable kinship with folk art, and it was this about Rousseau that impressed young artists who at the time were seeking new ways. But whereas their fondness for Primitive art came about as a highly conscious attitude, in Rousseau it was a sincere expression of his personality.

Rousseau was a self-taught artist. He was nicknamed the *Douanier* because for many years he worked for the local Paris customs office. He retired on a pension and began to paint when he was forty. An original and talented man full of childish confidence in himself and in the extent of his learning, he supported himself by teaching music, singing, declamation, and painting. From 1886 on he took part in the annual Salon des Indépendants, where the exhibits did not have to be approved by a jury. With the support of Cubists and Fauves he exhibited at the Salon d'Automne in 1905 and 1907.

HENRI ROUSSEAU

1844–1910

View of Montsouris Park

Oil on canvas, 18⅛ × 15″
Formerly Museum of Modern Western Art, Moscow

It is noteworthy that so ordinary a corner of the Paris park, a path between two fences, should have attracted Rousseau's attention. The somewhat comical combination of nursemaids in their pretty white caps and soldiers in their traditional red trousers is typical of Rousseau's style.

Every leaf on the trees, every board in the fences, has been meticulously reproduced. The dimensions are gradually reduced as we move into depth, in order to give a sense of receding space, but the figures on the path are not shown in perspective. This accounts for the incorrect proportions: the bushes, the fences, and the buildings are all too high in relation to the tiny silhouettes of the nurses and soldiers. And yet, for all its inexact proportions, this landscape conveys a sense of the monumental, which is characteristic of Henri Rousseau.

PIERRE BONNARD

1867–1947

First Day of Spring in the Country

Panel, oil on canvas; 11′ 11¾″ × 11′ 4⅝″
Formerly Museum of Modern Western Art, Moscow

The black pond in the foreground, full of shadows and reflections, introduces us into a fairylike landscape framed by large trees with downy, light-yellow foliage. The trees in the distance are still bare, and their brown trunks and branches stand out sharply against the horizon of bluish fields. Closer to the foreground, on the pale-green meadow, children are seen walking and picking flowers; a woman lies on the grass; at the right we glimpse a pair of lovers; pink and lavender blossoms are opening on the bushes.

The panel, dating from 1912, is executed in soft colors with a yellowish-pink dominant. With its decorative character, its fragile forms devoid of sharp contours, its high horizon line and absence of sky, it produces a tapestry-like effect.

PLATE 90

PIERRE BONNARD

1867–1947

Autumn: Fruit Picking

Panel, oil on canvas; $11' \ 11\frac{3}{4}'' \times 11' \ 4\frac{5}{8}''$
Formerly Museum of Modern Western Art, Moscow

The panel was commissioned by the famous collector, I. A. Morozov, for the lobby of his house in Moscow. It was conceived as a complement to the central panel, *On the Mediterranean Coast*, which dates from 1911 (now in The Hermitage). *Autumn*, painted a year later, *First Day of Spring in the Country*, and *Dance* (all three in the Museum) may be regarded as independent works.

Bonnard began as a poster designer and lithographer; he also painted stage sets. His early works show the influence of Toulouse-Lautrec. Later he joined the Neo-Impressionists (Denis, Vuillard, Roussel, etc.) who were influenced by Gauguin, and in 1892 formed a small group known as the Nabis. At that time he was fond of flat surfaces, contrasting tones, and clearly marked contours.

PLATE 91

PIERRE BONNARD

1867–1947

The Mirror in the Dressing Room

Oil on canvas, 47¼ × 38⅛″
Formerly Museum of Modern Western Art, Moscow

This composition, painted in 1908, is charming in color. A framed mirror hung above a dressing table with crockery of a nacreous bluish-white reflects the image of a chest of drawers and a nude seen from the back. The white body with warm, brilliant yellow accents contrasts with the cool blue of the bed and the grays of the crockery. The soft, predominantly blue curtain under the table contrasts with the translucent muslin curtain at the window. The forms are modeled by an interlacing of lines and brush strokes. This seemingly casual painting in a fairylike palette of silvery grays and subdued blues is a perfect example of the closed, intimate world so dear to Bonnard and Vuillard.

PLATE 92

ÉDOUARD VUILLARD

1869–1940

In the Garden

Tempera on cardboard, 20⅛ × 32⅝″
Formerly Museum of Modern Western Art, Moscow

About 1895 Vuillard painted a number of parks and gardens. The work shown here is closely related to the triptych *Aux Tuileries* (Musée d'Art Moderne, Paris), dated 1894, and was probably painted the same year. By raising the horizon line, Vuillard enlarges the space; the round flower bed enhances the effect of the composition. We seem to be taken into a hermetically closed grove, separated from the rest of the world by the thick foliage that casts its shadow on the ground. The impression of intimacy is strengthened by the serene atmosphere and total absence of movement.

Like many other Neo-Impressionists, Vuillard paints with small brush strokes and renounces balanced composition. The tendency to the decorative, already so marked in the last Impressionists, dominates his works. Nature is treated solely as an object of decorative explorations. The painter is interested above all in refined color harmonies. The yellow cardboard on which the picture is painted is not entirely covered; Vuillard uses it masterfully as an element of his palette and combines unpainted areas with small blue and white spots to produce the illusion of light and shadow. The contours of the color spots further accentuate the tendency to decorative synthesis. The matte surface results from the use of tempera.

PLATE 93

ALBERT MARQUET

1875–1947

Notre Dame in the Rain

Oil on canvas, 25⅝ × 31⅞″
Formerly Museum of Modern Western Art, Moscow

Unlike the Impressionists, Marquet re-creates the landscape and schematizes it, reducing it to artistic conciseness. Like an architect, with a sure and rapid hand, by means of long brush strokes and occasional color accents, he draws the plan of the landscape he sees.

The quays of the Seine, the dark area under the bridge, a tall building on the opposite bank, glistening sidewalks, Notre Dame in the distant mist, a few cabs, rare pedestrians in the rain—and this is Paris! No one else could have conveyed so simply and clearly that this is Paris in the rain, that the river is rising, and that there is a bit of sunshine on the Quai Bourbon. No one else could have so laconically and so firmly sketched a subject and breathed life into it.

Marquet loved Paris and knew it well. He went there in 1890, studied at the École des Arts Décoratifs, and in 1897 met Matisse and worked with him under Gustave Moreau at the École des Beaux-Arts. From 1905 on, he exhibited his works with the group of artists around Matisse that became known as the Fauves. Marquet, however, differs from most of the Fauves by his careful observation and rendering of reality. He traveled a great deal, painted waterfronts, and sea and river ports, and sketched street scenes and silhouettes of pedestrians.

In this painting Marquet uses an austere palette—black diagonals, glistening white areas, and a yellow-gray mist enveloping the cathedral in the distance. Marquet often painted this view from the windows of a house on the Quai Saint-Michel. For all their laconism and schematism, his landscapes are not devoid of lyricism. They are not lifeless schemata, mere photographs, but renderings of nature traced by an accomplished draftsman, executed by a subtle colorist, and keenly observed by an artist who loved reality in all its forms.

PLATE 94

GEORGES ROUAULT

1871–1958

Bathers

Watercolor and pastel on paper pasted on cardboard, 25⅝ × 36¼″
Formerly Museum of Modern Western Art, Moscow

This work was painted in 1907, two years after the famous exhibition that marked the emergence of Fauvism. Rouault was one of the Fauves, but from the outset he was distinguished by his striving to express his inner life in his paintings. His admiration for medieval stained-glass windows is reflected in his sonorous colors. He is closer to Expressionism than any other French painter of his generation.

In *Bathers* he distorts the actual forms of the human body and of the landscape to express his poetic perception of a specific moment of nature. Strange figures of women wade slowly in the water, stand motionless, or sit relaxed on the shore of the lake. The dynamic lines of the landscape, indicated by rapid brush strokes, and the intense colors, now flaring into sinister reds, violets, and greens, now dying down in gradations of blue ranging from a near-black to a tender pale blue, create the feeling that nature is shaken by convulsions that cause sky, sun, and water to swirl and then to subside in the slow, spellbound motions of the figures.

The whole picture produces an impression of weariness—as though nature, exhausted by her struggle with the onset of night, were making a last attempt to preserve the reality of her contours. But dusk is victorious, blurring forms and colors. Thus the artist transforms the ordinary change from day to night into an event full of hidden meaning—it is as though we were witnessing a mystery play about nature's agony.

PLATE 95

ANDRÉ DERAIN

1880–1954

Le Château

Oil on canvas, $32\frac{1}{8} \times 26''$ · Formerly Museum of Modern Western Art, Moscow

Derain played an important part in the development of modern painting. He was one of the originators of Fauvism, and later one of the first to discover the significance of Cézanne and Primitive art, and one of the earliest Cubists. However, he remained more faithful to nature than did the other Cubists.

He painted *Le Château* in 1910, when Picasso and Braque had begun to break up forms, passing to the second, so-called synthetic stage of Cubism. Derain stays within analytical Cubism, concentrating on volumes, and, unlike the other Cubists, preserving the reality of space and the brilliance of colors.

Against the dark-blue sky in the background, the motionless masses of the houses, as well as the bare trees and the massive hills, seem to grow organically from the soil. The aspects of the visible world are somewhat simplified and distorted, but they remain related to reality. The contrasts between saturated orange, blue, and green tones, and the austere, ponderous volumes convey a fairly accurate idea of the sun-parched landscape of southern France.

PLATE 96

MAURICE DE VLAMINCK

1876–1958

The River

Oil on canvas, $32\frac{5}{8} \times 40\frac{1}{8}''$ · Formerly Museum of Modern Western Art, Moscow

Vlaminck was born in Paris; his father was Flemish, and his ancestors were Dutch. He was always opposed to academic teaching and did not attend any art school. Derain, his friend, introduced him to Matisse; Vlaminck became one of the Fauves. As a young man he was interested in music as well as painting. He was also active as a writer and poet; he made tapestry cartoons and painted stage settings. He was strongly influenced by Van Gogh. His early landscapes and portraits are distinguished by their brilliant color.

About 1912 Vlaminck renounced the riotous colors of his Fauve period, confining himself to a palette of greenish-blues and grays. In *The River* the black water flows into the distance, the tree branches are shaken by the wind, and their agitation has a tragic quality. Isolated houses loom in the background. The colors are intense, gloomy.

The romantic mood of this work is in keeping with Vlaminck's conception of the landscape, which he defines as "an image of nature conveying the artist's mood." He also said that "objects are charged with lyricism." He held that the most important thing in an artist is temperament, instinct, that the visible world should be expressed without preconceived ideas, and that the artist must not paint what he sees with his eyes but what he feels, in order to express himself more fully. His ideas on art and his works are typical of the Neo-Romantic current of French painting in the 1930s and 1940s.

PLATE 97

HENRI MATISSE

1869–1954

The Artist's Studio

Oil on canvas, $71\frac{1}{4} \times 87\frac{1}{8}''$
Formerly Museum of Modern Western Art, Moscow

Matisse, who studied under Gustave Moreau at the École des Beaux-Arts, was first inspired by the old masters he copied in The Louvre. Later his palette brightened, and he painted in the Impressionist and Neo-Impressionist manners. From 1905 on he exhibited his works with the Fauves (Vlaminck, Marquet, Derain, etc.), of whom he was the leader. In this period he employs brilliant, contrasting colors in bold decorative compositions. His interiors, still lifes, landscapes, and portraits express triumphant joy. He did not aim at complete faithfulness to reality, nor did he ignore it. He schematized reality, using a deliberately simplified drawing.

In *The Artist's Studio* of 1911, however, he renounces the use of exaggerated color contrasts. The colors are still sonorous, but now they are harmonized. It is interesting to note, for instance, the gradation of the various greens: the decorative motif on the rusty-colored vase at the left, the dark-green pad on the brown chest, the green meadow in the painting hung on the wall (*La Volupté*, 1907/08), the joyful foliage outside the window, the greenish shadows on the plaster cast, and the dark-green vase at the right, next to the panel, *Dance*. There is also the green screen at the center with a dark-blue fabric thrown over it. The small green pitcher in front of the screen is, so to speak, the key to the whole decorative composition, which breathes lightness, freshness, and joy. A certain spatial element is introduced by the yellow rug disposed diagonally on the pink floor, the high lavender wall, and the slanting legs of the stands. The artist once again respects reality: this painting anticipates the style of his postwar works.

Matisse treated the theme of the studio in a number of other paintings. The Museum of Modern Art in New York owns a panel entitled *Red Studio*, which shows the left part of the same room. A preliminary watercolor study for this painting is in the Print Room of the Pushkin Museum.

PLATE 98

HENRI MATISSE

1869–1954

Nasturtiums and the Panel "Dance"

Oil on canvas, 75½ × 44⅞"
Formerly Museum of Modern Western Art, Moscow

Matisse frequently treated the subject of dance; it turns up for the first time as a secondary detail in *La Joie de vivre* of 1907 (Barnes Collection in Merion, Pennsylvania). Later we find a panel showing a dance in some of Matisse's interiors—for instance, *Fruits, Flowers, and Panel* (1909, The Hermitage) and *The Artist's Studio* (1911, Pushkin Museum). But it is in the *Dance* of 1910 (The Hermitage) that the motif—a swirl of bodies in movement—achieves its fullest expression.

Each time he paints a dance, Matisse creates new harmonies. He composes an intricate chromatic symphony, enlarging or contracting space, and altering the contours of the figures. The *Nasturtiums*, painted in 1912, shows only the left side of a panel which fills the entire background. Although the blue harmonizes with the reddish-pink bodies, it is strikingly brilliant. The bold diagonal of the blue-black plinth forms a demarcation line between the blue of the wall and the blue of the floor, each of a different shade. The raspberry-red stand and pitcher, the green leaves of the nasturtiums, the raspberry-red armchair with the striped seat intensify the colors without slowing the movement of the dance.

The painting is vertical, so that the figures are elongated, whereas in the large *Dance* they are as though compressed by the horizontal format of the panel. Here the contours of the figures are more elegant, they seem to be flying, hovering in the blueness, having lost all support, freed from gravity.

Matisse returned to the theme several years later. In the most famous variation, a panel executed for Barnes in 1933, the figures are even more schematic. The panel is like a gigantic ornamental fresco, and the colors reflect a certain "aestheticism," having lost the brilliance of the earlier dances.

PLATE 99

PABLO PICASSO

1881–

Girl on a Ball

Oil on canvas, $55\frac{1}{2} \times 37\frac{3}{8}''$
Formerly Museum of Modern Western Art, Moscow

During his so-called Pink Period (1904–06) Picasso treated the same subjects as in the preceding years—traveling circus performers, beggars, common people—but his palette changed. The colors became lighter, more transparent; the contours more harmonious and more fluid. The tragic mood of the earlier works gave way to tenderness and lyricism.

The painting shown here, dating from 1904, is the masterpiece of the Pink Period. The fragile body of the girl intent on keeping her balance contrasts with the motionless, heavy figure of the athlete. However, although the two figures are so different from each other that it is scarcely possible to imagine that they have anything in common, this painting does not suggest the sense of solitude and isolation of beings that characterizes Picasso's earlier works. The color scheme is based on simple pinks and blues, given in complex relationships almost as ungraspable as the subtlest shades of human emotions. The blues and reddish-pinks of the male figure are harsh; the blue-grays and ashy pinks of the girl's complexion and costume are softer; and in the background these colors dissolve into a kind of bluish-pink mist.

These tender colors, by creating the lyrical mood that unifies the figures, suggest their common lot. The circus performers of the earlier works here seem to turn to each other. Sensing their spiritual affinity, they achieve a precarious moment of inner balance.

PLATE 100

PABLO PICASSO

1881–

Majorcan Woman

Tempera and watercolor on cardboard, $26\frac{3}{8} \times 20\frac{1}{8}''$
Formerly Museum of Modern Western Art, Moscow

This intriguing work dates from 1905, that is, from Picasso's Pink Period.
It shows a girl wearing a strange headdress, her head slightly turned; she seems to be listening to something or to be absorbed in her own thoughts. Broad strokes of blue surround the figure; hands, clothing, and facial features are indicated by light-gray lines. The exquisite combinations of browns and cool blues, and the lines of the drawing, at once soft and fragile, felicitously supplement the pure, somewhat melancholy beauty of the figure. This beauty has the transparency of a dream. The warm brown area of the body is an unpainted section of the cardboard, whose color is the same as that of the light areas in the background. This girl is created out of nothing, she is like a ghost, a fragile negative of reality—she is even less real than the homogeneous cool blue of the space around her.

In this, as in many other works of the Pink Period, Picasso strives to capture the mirage of beauty. He captures it for a moment, recording its colors with rapid brush strokes, but the image has no consistency, it is ready to vanish, to dissolve in a cold and hostile world. It is perhaps this feeling that beauty is unstable, ephemeral in our contemporary world, which accounts for the mood of lyrical melancholy characteristic of the Pink Period.